UNUSUALLY FUN

GRADE 3

READING & MATH

SERIOUSLY FUN TOPICS TO TEACH SERIOUSLY IMPORTANT SKILLS

Carson Dellosa Education
Greensboro, North Carolina

The facts presented in this book are for informational and entertainment purposes only. The nature of extreme facts makes them difficult to authenticate. Carson Dellosa Education makes no warranty as to the reliability, accuracy, timeliness, usefulness, or completeness of the facts contained herein.

Credits
Authors: Jennifer Stith, Hailey Scragg, Catherine Malaski
Cover Design: Joshua Janes
Interior Design: Joshua Janes, Lynne Schwaner

Carson Dellosa Education
PO Box 35665
Greensboro, NC 27425
carsondellosa.com

© 2023, Carson Dellosa Education. The purchase of this material entitles the buyer to reproduce worksheets and activities for classroom use only—not for commercial resale. Reproduction of these materials for an entire school or district is prohibited. No part of this book may be reproduced (except as noted above), stored in a retrieval system, or transmitted in any form or by any means (mechanically, electronically, recording, etc.) without the prior written consent of Carson Dellosa Education.

Printed in the USA • All rights reserved.
01-191237784

ISBN 978-1-4838-6712-0

TABLE OF CONTENTS

Astonishing Animals and Plants

Square Poop? Really?...........................4
Fainting Goats 8
One Smart Plant.................................12
Tasty Tears.......................................16
Funky Feet..20
Bini the Bunny 24
March of the Ducks............................28
Costumed Crabs 32
A Tree of Many Colors.........................36
Can-Do Kangaroos.............................40
Brainy Bees 44
Think Pink...48
Koko Meets Mr. Rogers 52
Stubbs for Mayor 56

Curious Customs

Bawling Babies...................................60
A Very Cheesy Sport 64
Dining on Dog Food 68
Hamburger Harry................................72
Celebrating Socks..............................76
Wacky Laws 80
Sleeping on the Job 84
Beachcombing for Toys 88
Rotten Teeth 92
High Heel History 96
Sniff This!...100
Toothy Traditions 104

Awesome Anatomy

Tongue Twisted..................................108
Gassy Facts......................................112
Growing in Space 116
Turning Orange..................................120
Amazing Earwax.................................124
Baby Bones 128

Odd Objects

Bubble Gum Broccoli 132
Bet You Can! 136
Totally Toque 140
Perfect Pizza 144
Accidental Invention...........................148
Grandma's Fruitcake 152
Fairy Floss 156
Yellow Means Stop..............................160
Ketchup as Medicine 164
Whatchamacallit?...............................168
Pecan Pie 24/7 172
Wacky Warnings.................................176

Peculiar Places

"Highest Court" 180
Rockin' Roads....................................184
Pink Lakes...188
Tree House Villages 192
Icehotel...196
A Town with No Name 200
Pig Island..204
Ice Cream Graveyard 208
House of Mugs...................................212

Answer Key 216

SQUARE POOP? REALLY?

Yes, bare-nosed wombats really do make square nuggets when they poop! They are marsupials and live in Australia. They're about as big as a border collie and they waddle when they walk.

Because their poop is 3D, they are actually cube shaped, not square. They make six to eight at a time. They are about 2 centimeters (0.8 inches) and they can push out about 100 a day!

WOMBAT
CUBE DISPENSER
CLAWS FOR DIGGING
BARE NOSE
SHORT LEGS

FUN FACT Wombats take about two weeks to digest their meals of roots, grass, and bark.

WOMBAT SQUARE POOP

That's a lot of poop. But wombats put it to good use. Square poop is more useful than round poop. The cube shape keeps them from rolling away. Wombats stack them on rocks and logs—the higher the better. That's how they mark their territory. This tells predators to stay away. It gets the attention of other wombats. No other animal in the world drops square poo. Wombats are one of a kind!

Complete each sentence with a word from the word bank.

| cube | intestines | marsupials |

1. A wombat's _____ are responsible for their poo's unique shape.

2. Wombats, kangaroos, and opossums are all _____.

3. A _____ is a 3D figure that has square faces.

Write a response to each question.

4. What is the main idea or topic of this passage?

_____

_____

5. How does the shape of a wombat's poop help them?

_____

_____

6. What text feature did you notice? How did it add to the story?

_____

_____

_____

Circle the answer.

1. Which poop could have been made by a wombat? Explain why.

_____

Solve each problem.

2. In the morning, the wombat at the zoo creates 21 cubes. By lunch, he creates 36 more cubes. So far, how many cubes has he created in all?

_____ cubes

3. A zookeeper sees 4 piles of poop on Monday. She sees another 4 piles of poop on Tuesday. If the pattern continues, how many piles of poop would she see by Friday?

_____ piles

Follow the directions.

Read all the clues. Color the box red if the clue doesn't match. Color the box green if it does match. The first box has been colored for you.

Three wombats made their morning poo piles. Which pile belongs to each wombat?

- Wilma's pile is the biggest.
- Wally's pile is smaller than Wilma's.
- Wendy's pile has an even number of poo cubes.

Explain your answer. _____

FAINTING GOATS

Warning: The following passage is not for the faint-of-heart. Just kid-ing. A little goat humor for you.

Fainting goats, wooden-leg goats, stiff-leg goats, and scare-goats are just a few nicknames given to a specific breed of goat. These goats have a genetic condition called *myotonia* (my-uh-toe-nee-uh) *congenita*. This muscular condition causes the goats to tense up when they are startled. Because the goats fall over, the name fainting goats is commonly used.

FUN FACT Goats' eyes have rectangular pupils. A rectangular pupil focuses on the horizon. This feature allows them to see predators that may be lurking in the distance.

With the growing popularity of watching funny animal videos on YouTube, fainting goats are a popular hit. You might want to laugh or you might feel baaaa-d for the goats. But know this—the condition is not harmful to the goats. They are just as healthy and playful as other goats.

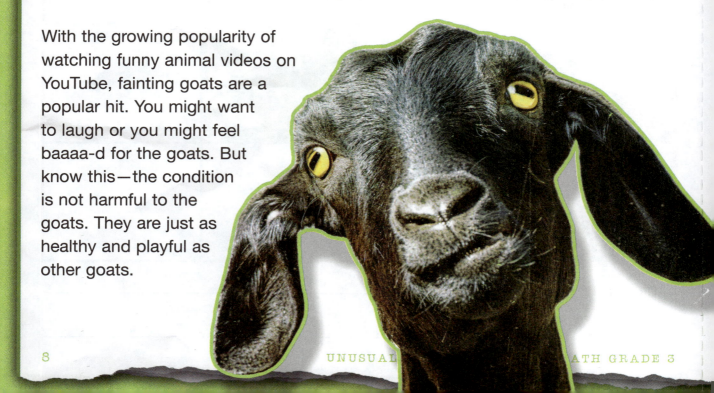

Answer each question.

1. What is the main idea of the passage?

   A. Goats have rectangular pupils.

   B. These goats have a condition that makes them fall over.

   C. Some goats have nicknames.

2. Which detail supports the main idea?

   A. A goat's muscles tense when startled.

   B. The goats are just as healthy as other goats.

   C. Fainting goat videos are popular.

Write a response to each question.

3. What is the author's purpose for writing this passage?
   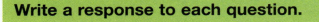

4. What nicknames are given to this breed of goat? Think of a new nickname for this breed of goat and write it above the goat.

_____

_____

Solve each problem.

1. Farmer Day is building a rectangular pen for his goats. The area where he is building the pen is 72 square feet. How much fencing does Farmer Day need to buy if one side of the fencing is 8 feet long?

   _____ feet of fencing

2. If Farmer Day decides to divide the area in half, then what would the area be in one half?

   _____ square feet

Circle the answers.

3. Goats' eyes have rectangular pupils. Which of the figures below are rectangles?

Write a response to the question.

4. How do you know the figures are rectangles? Explain.

   _____
   _____
   _____

Use the code to answer the question.

Question: Why was the barn so noisy?

Answer: Because,

ONE SMART PLANT

Whether it appears to you as a yucky pile of worms or a brain, the brain cactus's name fits this cool plant. This succulent is native to Mexico. It is a rare form of a cactus called *Mammillaria Elongata,* commonly known as Lady Fingers, which grows upright. But, why does the cactus sometimes form a brain-like appearance?

The wave-like crests of the brain cactus most likely started from damage to the baby plant. All succulents have a center of growth. This center is called the *apical meristem*. If this area is chewed by an insect or crushed by a passing animal, the cactus is likely to grow abnormally. More rarely, a mutation, or change, can happen in the cells of the plant while it is growing. The stems grow in waves instead of upwards.

Like most cacti, the brain cactus is easy to care for. It needs lots of light, little water, and well-draining soil. And if the cactus needs to be repotted, a planter in the shape of a head is a fine choice.

FUN FACT — The cockscomb flower can also have a brain-like appearance. Funny enough, it has been used in medicines to treat headaches.

Answer each question.

1. Which is the meaning of the word crest in the passage?

   A. the tuft on a bird's head

   B. a coat of arms

   C. the top of a wave

2. What is an *apical meristem*?

   A. flower

   B. center of growth on a cactus

   C. spike on a cactus

3. Which is not needed for a cactus to grow?

   A. lots of light

   B. shelter

   C. well-draining soil

Write a response to each question.

4. What could have happened to the cactus to make it look like a brain?

   _____

   _____

5. How does the author feel about the brain cactus?

   _____

UNUSUALLY FUN READING & MATH GRADE 3

Solve each problem.

Succulent	Price	50% off Sundays
Jade	$7.00	
Brain Cactus	$3.00	
Aloe	$2.00	
Burrito Sedum	$5.00	
String of Pearls	$9.00	
Desert Rose	$6.00	

1. Sandy's Succulents Garden Center sells only succulents. Look at the price list. If you have $20 to spend at the garden center, what could you buy?

_____

_____

_____

2. On Sundays, Sandy discounts her succulents. She offers each plant at 50% off. Write the discounted price of each plant in the table above.

Use the information in the table to write your own problem. Solve it.

3. _____

_____

_____

Follow the multiples of 2 through the brain cactus maze.

TASTY TEARS

Ever get a craving for something sweet? How about something salty? Most cravings happen when our bodies need a certain nutrient. This happens to other animals too.

"DEW" DROP IN!

When we picture butterflies, we see fluttering insects flying from flower to flower drinking up sweet nectar. What we don't think of is a butterfly drinking from the eyes of a turtle or other animal. But it happens. This behavior is called lachryphagy (lah-CRIH-fih-ge). Tear-drinking butterflies are in search of sodium. If they can't get sodium from water sources such as puddles, they are bound to find some in the salty tears of a turtle or caiman (a relative of an alligator).

Butterflies taste with their feet, but they drink with a long straw-like proboscis. After finding a salty sip butterflies extend their proboscis into the eyes of animals and slurp sodium, proteins, and other nutrients. The host animal is not harmed and the butterflies satisfy their needs.

FUN FACT

Humans are the only animals that cry when upset. But all animals produce tears. Tears keep eyes moist, washing away dirt and other harmful materials.

Complete each sentence with a word from the word bank.

| sodium | nectar | proboscis | nutrient |

1. Tears contain _____ which gives tears their salty taste.

2. A butterfly drinks with a straw-like tube called a _____.

3. Protein is one _____ found in tears.

4. Flowers contain a sweet liquid called _____.

Write a response to each question.

5. What does the author write about the relationship between a butterfly and the animals whose tears they drink?

_____

_____

_____

6. The behavior of tear-drinking is called lachryphagy. In Greek, the word *phagos* means one that eats. What do you think the first part of the word means? Use a dictionary to check your answer.

_____

_____

THIRST QUENCHER

CAVE OF NO RETURN

UNUSUALLY FUN RE

17

Solve each problem.

1. Ty Turtle had 55 butterflies drink from his tears this week. Casey Caiman had 76 butterflies drink from his tears this week. Who had more butterflies? How much more?

_____ had _____ more butterflies drink his tears.

2. Tina, Tara, and Toby are soaking up the sun. Along come some butterflies. If each turtle has 6 butterflies land to drink from their tears, how many butterflies landed on the turtles in all?

_____ butterflies

3. Cara Caiman begins her morning swim. She sees 24 butterflies drinking tears from her 2 friends' eyes. Write three different number sentences to show how many butterflies could be on each friend.

Trace each path to find out which butterfly drank from the turtle's eyes.

FUNKY FEET

EAU DE CORN CHIPS

PROTEUS

PSEUDOMONAS

FUZZY WUZZY FACE

Leash? Check. Dog food? Check. Odor? Check.

From the sweet scent of puppy breath to the gag-inducing pile of dog poo, the range of smells is vast for any new dog owner. One strange smell that dog-owners are often curious about is the faint smell of corn chips wafting from their pooch's paws.

Known as "Frito feet," dog owners describe paws as smelling like a popular brand of corn chips. What is going on here? Just like on human skin, dog's paws have bacteria and fungus. Because dogs don't often wear shoes outside, they pick up all sort of organisms on their pads. Two of the bacteria known to live on paws are called *Pseudomonas* and *Proteus*. These bacteria give off a yeasty odor similar to a popular corn chip snack. Mmmm. Anyone have some salsa?

FUN FACT Just like humans show handedness (lefty vs. righty) some dogs show a paw preference.

Answer each question.

1. According to the text, on which part of a dog's paw would you find the bacteria that causes "Frito feet"?

    A. claw

    B. pad

    C. fur

2. Which words in the text mean the same as *smell*?

    A. odor

    B. chips

    C. scent

Write a response to each question.

3. What does the author explain is the cause of Frito feet?

   _____

   _____

4. Do your feet smell like corn chips? Think of three words that describe how your feet smell. Label the foot with the words.

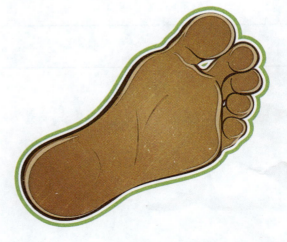

Write four numbers that when added equal the number in the paw.

1. 16
2. 24
3. 35

Write a response to each question.

4. Dan's dog left muddy footprints all over the house. Dan counts the footprints by 4s and counts a total of 44 footprints. Which numbers would Dan say aloud as he counts?

_____

_____

5. Dan's sister Daisy counts the footprints by 2s. She counts a total of 43. Explain why her total is incorrect.

_____

_____

_____

Find and circle 10 words that name parts of a dog.

```
E N O S E J D R C V
K Y M U Z Z L E P F
N Z S V W G M R A Y
T U G F I E S A D W
A P Z Q T F A H K H
I P A W H U L R X I
L Q O H E I E G K S
J E P G R Q G I T K
E Z Y N S E U B Z E
F X T C L A W M J R
```

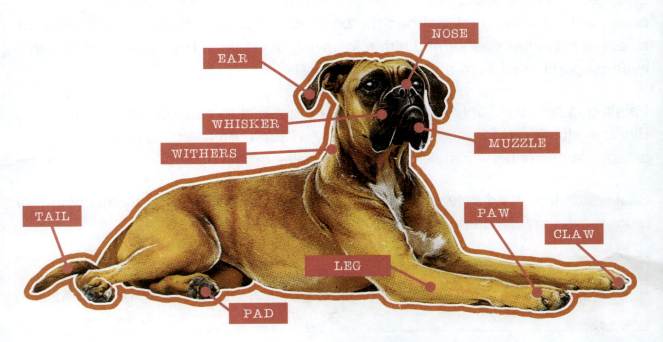

BINI THE BUNNY

Do you think that rabbits are all fluff and no stuff? Well, Bini the bunny will prove you wrong. This Holland Lop Rabbit has created quite a social media following with his unique tricks and talents. Bini's owner, Shai Asor, recognized early on that Bini was special.

*DUE TO SCHEDULING ISSUES, BINI IS BEING PLAYED BY HIS FAMOUS STUNT DOUBLE, BUNNY BILLY, FOR THE ABOVE PHOTO.

One day, Bini got into some markers and left a mess. Instead of being mad, Shai decided to encourage Bini's artistry and offered him some paint brushes, paint, and a canvas. Bini grabbed the brushes and began to paint. Bini's blend of colors and strokes has earned him a following of art fans. His masterpieces can even be purchased from his own online store!

Painting is not Bini's only talent. Shai has taught Bini to play basketball, earning Bini a world record for most slam dunks by a rabbit. Bini also plays pool and arcade games and even styles and combs hair—or is it hare!?

Shai wants the world to know how smart rabbits are. He is currently teaching Bini more tricks that will demonstrate his intellect.

FUN FACT Save the carrots for your salad! Carrots can give rabbits an upset stomach if they eat too many.

Write two different meanings for each word from the passage.

1. pool

2. left

Answer the question.

3. How did Bini's owner feel when Bini made a mess with the markers?

A. He was mad and never let Bini make art again.

B. He was happy and let Bini color on anything he wanted to.

C. He turned Bini's interest in coloring into a positive by giving Bini painting materials.

Write a response to the question.

4. Shai says that he wants to show the world how smart rabbits are. If you were Bini's owner, what trick or skill would you teach him next? Why?

Look at each number line. Write an equation to match.

1.

   _____ × _____ = _____

2.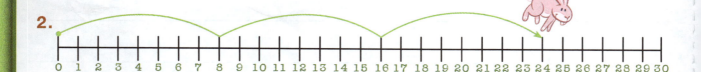

   _____ × _____ = _____

Look at each equation. Show it on the number line.

3. 2 × 11 = 22

4. 5 × 5 = 25

Follow the directions.

Color the numbered sections in the order below to reveal a special treat just for Bini.

1. Color **orange** the numbers you say when you count by 10s.

2. Color **blue** the remaining even numbers.

3. Color **green** the numbers you say when you count by 5s.

4. Color **purple** the remaining odd numbers.

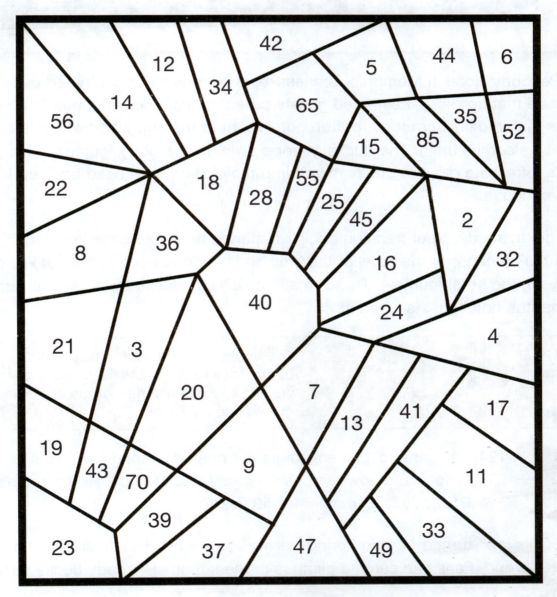

UNUSUALLY FUN READING & MATH GRADE 3

MARCH OF THE DUCKS

The Peabody Hotel in Memphis, Tennessee, is famous for its feathered guests. You read that correctly. Feathered guests called ducks. These famous Peabody Ducks march daily from their rooftop hotel room to the lobby below where a red carpet welcomes them. The ducks go for a swim in the lobby fountain. Then, after a refreshing dip, the ducks march into the elevator and head back up to the penthouse.

How did this red-carpet tradition begin? It started as a joke back in the 1930s when the manager of the hotel at the time and his duck-hunting pal put live duck decoys in the hotel fountain. Three small English call ducks were used. It turns out that the hotel guests loved it!

FUN FACT

The ducks work only for three months before they return to the farm where they were raised. Then, a new group of ducks moves into the hotel.

In 1940, a former circus animal trainer offered to train the ducks to perform the now famous Peabody Duck March. He served as the Peabody Duckmaster for 50 years.

This joke-turned-tradition brings visitors to the hotel from all over the world. Fans can catch a glimpse of the famous Peabody ducks daily.

Answer each question.

1. What is one thing that makes the Peabody Hotel famous?

    A. its lobby fountain

    B. its resident ducks

    C. its elevator

2. How did the red-carpet tradition begin?

    A. as a joke

    B. to show that the hotel is pet-friendly

    C. to show how easy it is to train ducks

Write a response to each question.

3. In your opinion, do you think ducks are easy to train? Explain.

    _____

    _____

    _____

4. What skills do you think a Duckmaster needs to train ducks?

    _____

    _____

    _____

UNUSUALLY FUN READING & MATH GRADE 3   29

Solve each problem.

1. If the ducks spend time in the fountain from 11:00 am to 5:00 pm each day, how many hours do they swim in the fountain?

    _____ hours

2. If the ducks march every day from their hotel room to the fountain and back to their room, how many trips do they make in a week? In a 30-day month?

    _____ trips in a week   _____ trips in a month

Answer each question.

3. If the ducks were first placed into the fountain in 1933 and the Duckmaster began training ducks in 1940, how many years were ducks without a trainer?

    A. 7

    B. 17

    C. 8

PUTTING IN THE HOURS

4. Each duck works 3 months out of the year. How many rotations of ducks does the hotel do in one year?

    A. 12

    B. 9

    C. 4

Follow the directions.

You are hired as the new Duckmaster. Help the ducks march through the hotel. Color the boxes whose sums are multiples of 10.

GO				
16 + 34	17 + 13	51 + 9	41 + 18	33 + 53
42 + 26	19 + 10	45 + 25	57 + 22	20 + 13
85 + 14	84 + 6	32 + 18	13 + 44	15 + 12
41 + 57	28 + 42	56 + 31	54 + 24	64 + 23
75 + 13	33 + 67	19 + 31	46 + 14	25 + 25 STOP

UNUSUALLY FUN READING & MATH GRADE 3

COSTUMED CRABS

Ever see a dog in a costume? How about a crab? No? Well, if you swim in the Red Sea you might catch a glimpse of one. A carrier crab, or urchin crab, has a unique taste in headgear.

Carrier crabs move about the sea floor on only two pairs of their legs. The other pairs of legs are too busy carrying a sea urchin. The sea urchin doesn't mind though. It has the chance to be moved around to different feeding grounds.

FUN FACT Carrier crabs have also been observed carrying sea sponges and coral.

So, why does the carrier crab take this "friend" for a ride? For protection of course! Carrier crabs are small at only 2 inches (5.08 cm) in length. This makes them easy prey for predators. Sea urchins have pointy spikes and the crabs know that fish won't attempt to eat something so spiky. Pretty good disguise, huh?

Answer each question.

1. The meaning of the word *taste* in the text is the same as which sentence?

    A. You have good taste in music.

    B. Would you like a taste of my dessert?

    C. I taste too much salt in this meal.

2. Why do carrier crabs use only their two front pairs of legs to move?

    A. They don't like the feel of the ocean floor.

    B. Their other legs are being used to carry something.

    C. Their other legs are missing.

Write a response to each question.

3. What might be a different title for this passage?

_____

4. How does the author describe the relationship between a carrier crab and a sea urchin?

_____

_____

_____

_____

_____

Solve each problem.

1. A scuba diver sees five carrier crabs carrying urchins along the sea floor. How many legs does the diver see? (Hint: Each crab has 10 legs, but it uses 4 legs to walk and the rest to carry an urchin.)

   _____ legs

2. A scuba diver sees 16 carrier crabs, but only 12 sea urchins. How many carrier crabs are not carrying an urchin?

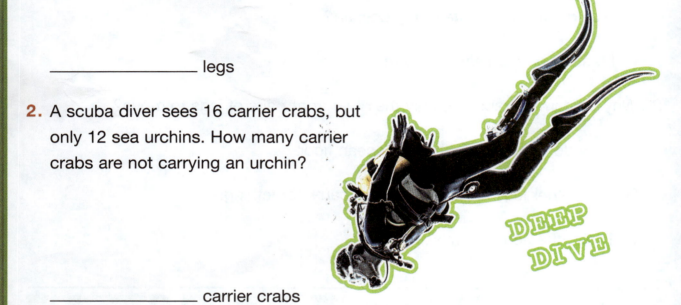

   _____ carrier crabs

Draw a picture to show the answer.

3. There are 10 urchins on the sea floor. Carrier crabs come along and carry away some of the urchins. Some urchins are left behind. How many different ways can you show this as a math equation?
   (Hint: Think of ways to show 10.)

Follow the directions.

Help the carrier crab hide in your room. Look around. Draw an object on its "head" that it could use to protect itself. Write a sentence describing your costumed crab.

A TREE OF MANY COLORS

Neon green, bright red, orange, blue, purple, and pink. Sounds like the colors in a box of crayons don't they? But, in fact, these are the colors of a unique tree called the rainbow eucalyptus.

As the tree sheds its bark, the layer underneath is a neon green. Once exposed to air the new layer ages, turns a different color, and sheds. With so many different parts of the tree in different stages of aging and shedding, the result is a beautiful array of rainbow colors.

A tropical forest with lots of rain is the best place to find this massive tree, such as those in the Philippines, New Guinea, and Indonesia. This is the only eucalyptus tree to grow naturally in the northern hemisphere. Rainbow eucalyptus trees are fast growers! They grow up to three feet per year and can reach a height of 250 feet (76 m).

FUN FACT

The thin layers of bark from the rainbow eucalyptus are often used for pulpwood. Pulpwood is the main ingredient in paper. You would think the paper would be colorful, but it is white.

Write two different meanings for each word from the passage.

1. bark: _____

_____

2. shed: _____

_____

Answer each question.

3. What reason does the author give to explain why the tree has so many colors?

   A. The tree sheds its bark, the bark underneath ages.

   B. The layer underneath the bark is rainbow colored.

   C. The bark that is shed turns colors when it falls to the ground.

4. Which statement is false?

   A. Rainbow eucalyptus trees can be found in the Philippines.

   B. Rainbow eucalyptus trees grow in dry climates.

   C. Rainbow eucalyptus trees are fast growers.

Write a response to the question.

5. What is the author's purpose for writing this passage?

_____

Solve each problem.

1. Dr. Root is studying young rainbow eucalyptus trees. He measures the trunk lengths of three young trees. Tree A is 3 feet 4 inches tall. Tree B is 49 inches tall. Tree C is 3 feet 11 inches tall. Order the trees from shortest to tallest.

_____ _____ _____

shortest ———————————————→ tallest

2. How much taller is the tallest tree than the shortest tree?

_____ inches

3. If the trees grow eight inches in a month, then how tall will each tree be at the end of the month?

Tree A: _____

Tree B: _____

Tree C: _____

Follow the directions.

Write numbers in each space. The number in each space is the sum of the two numbers below it.

1.

2.

CAN-DO KANGAROOS

What can a kangaroo do? Hop of course. What can't a kangaroo do? Walk backwards.

A kangaroo's body is designed for hopping forward at average speeds of 15 miles per hour (24.1 km/h). Their front legs are short and their back legs are long. Kangaroos move about by hopping on their huge feet and thick, muscular tail. The tail is often thought of as a kangaroo's third leg. It helps a kangaroo jump long distances—even as far as 30 feet (9.1 m) in one hop!

JUMP! JUMP! JUMP!

FUN FACT

A kangaroo joey, later named Doodlebug, was found abandoned near the side of a road in southeastern Australia. With no mom to offer a safe pouch, Doodlebug found security from a different animal—a stuffed animal teddy bear.

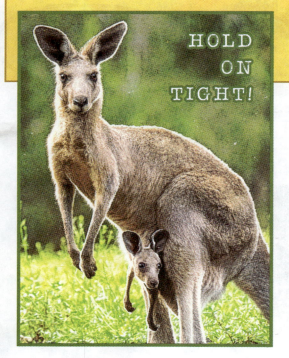

HOLD ON TIGHT!

What else can a kangaroo do? Jump while carrying a baby kangaroo, that's what! Kangaroos are marsupials. A kangaroo has a fur pouch that holds its joey after it is born. Joeys are born the size of a jelly bean. They stay in their mother's pouches for several months as they grow. Once a joey is old enough to leave the pouch, it may return only to feed or for security.

Complete each sentence with a word from the word bank.

average	pouch	security

1. Doodlebug found _____ from a teddy bear.

2. A kangaroo can hop at an _____ speed of 15 mph (24.1 km/h).

3. The joey stayed in his mother's _____ until he was too big.

Write a response to each question.

4. What is a *joey*?

_____

_____

5. What parts of a kangaroo help it jump?

_____

_____

Draw a picture to show each word's or phrase's meaning.

6. *third leg*

7. *jelly bean*

Use each number line to solve the problems.

1. A kangaroo hopped a distance of 50 feet. If each jump was 10 feet long, how many jumps did the kangaroo make?

2. Another kangaroo hopped a distance of 45 feet. If each jump was 5 feet long, how many jumps did the kangaroo make?

Use the table to solve each problem. (Use a calculator if needed.)

Age	Length	Weight
0 months (birth)	1 inch	1 ounce
adult	3 feet	84 pounds

3. How much longer is an adult kangaroo than it was at birth? (Hint: 12 inches = 1 foot)

_____

4. Write the number sentence you would use to find out the weight in ounces of an adult kangaroo. (Hint: 1 pound = 16 ounces)

_____ × _____ = _____

Follow the directions.

Question: How do kangaroos stay cool in temperatures of more than 100 degrees Fahrenheit?

Round each number to the nearest ten. Match each answer with the correct letter in the key. Write the letters in order on the lines.

1. 594 _____
2. 455 _____
3. 1,723 _____
4. 2,787 _____

Round each number to the nearest hundred. Match each answer with the correct letter in the key. Write the letters in order on the lines.

5. 886 _____
6. 842 _____
7. 657 _____
8. 3,179 _____
9. 1,920 _____
10. 6,059 _____
11. 4,846 _____
12. 7,217 _____

Key
590 = L
2,790 = K
460 = I
1,720 = C
1,900 = A
6,100 = R
700 = R
900 = F
4,800 = M
3,200 = E
7,200 = S
800 = O

COOL IS MY MIDDLE NAME.

WELL... ACTUALLY IT'S LEROY.

Answer:

THEY ____ ____ ____ ____

THEIR

____ ____ ____ ____ ____ ____ ____ .

UNUSUALLY FUN READING & MATH GRADE 3

BRAINY BEES

THE BRILLIANT & HUMBLE BUMBLE

What do bees know about math? A lot. A scientist in Australia, Dr. Scarlett Howard, is teaching honeybees to add, subtract, and understand the concept of zero.

How does she do this? Howard teaches one bee at a time. The bee is placed inside a Y maze, which is a covered box in the shape of the letter Y. The bee enters at the bottom of the Y and sees a math problem (a card printed with a number of shapes in one of two colors). For example, blue shapes mean add 1 and yellow shapes mean subtract 1. At the split of the Y, two answers await. If the bee chooses the correct path, it is rewarded with a treat.

Like with most animal training, Howard uses a reward system. The honeybees are rewarded with sugar water for correct answers and tonic water, which the bees find bitter, for incorrect answers. Now that's buzzworthy news to take back to the hive.

FUN FACT — Bees must know geometry too because the cells of their honeycombs are six-sided shapes, or hexagons.

Answer each question.

1. What is Dr. Howard teaching honeybees?

   A. How to find honey

   B. How to do math

   C. How to move through a maze

2. Which of the following could be one of the cards?

   A.    B.    C.

Write a response to the question.

3. How was Dr. Howard able to train the bees?

   _____

   _____

   _____

   _____

Draw each answer.

1. A bee is shown a card that has 5 yellow dots. (Remember that yellow means *subtract 1*.) What might the correct answer card look like?

2. A bee is shown a card that has 3 blue squares. (Remember that blue means *add 1*.) What might the correct answer card look like?

Solve each problem.

3.
```
  24        76        84        59
- 16      + 25      - 61      - 40
```

4.
```
  677       409       783       226
+ 486     + 304     - 250     + 102
```

Help the honeybee find the flower by coloring the multiples of 3.

THINK PINK

A pink animal often elicits an "Ooh," "Aww," or a "How Cute!" response. But, being pink is rare in the animal kingdom. To visitors adventuring to the Amazon in Peru, a sighting of one particular pink animal is an amazing experience.

The boto, or pink river dolphin, is a species of freshwater dolphin found throughout the Amazon River. Botos are born gray but take on a pink hue as they age. Males are pinker than females and when a boto is excited, it turns even pinker—just like when you blush!

PRETTY

Botos are shy and elusive, often traveling alone or in small groups. They spend lots of time underwater only peeking their heads up once in a while. What is interesting is that these dolphins are curious and outgoing around humans. They may even play alongside the small boats of people out to explore the wonders of the Amazon.

IN PINK

FUN FACT: Botos can be seen swimming upside down! They turn quickly by using one flipper to swim forward and the other to swim backward.

Complete each sentence with a word from the word bank.

hue	rare	elusive

1. Seeing a boto is _____ making it a very special experience if you do see one.

2. Adult botos have a deeper pink _____ than baby botos.

3. Often found traveling alone, botos can be shy and _____.

Write a response to each question.

4. What does the author say is interesting?

_____

_____

_____

5. Do you agree? Explain.

_____

_____

_____

Solve each problem.

1. Tito's Tours went out on the Amazon River each day of the week Monday–Friday. On Monday, the boat of tourists saw 4 botos. If each day they saw one more boto than the day before, how many botos did they see that week?

_____ botos

2. Boto Boat Tours went out on the Amazon River each day of the week Monday–Friday. On Monday, the boat of tourists saw 11 botos. If they saw one less boto each day the boat went out, how many botos did they see that week?

_____ botos

Complete each table.

3. In one month, Tito's Tours saw a total of 36 botos. If they saw the same amount of botos each week, how many did they see each week?

Week 1	_____ botos
Week 2	_____ botos
Week 3	_____ botos
Week 4	_____ botos
	Total = 36 botos

4. In one month, Boto Boat Tours saw a total of 80 botos. If they saw the same amount of botos each week, how many did they see each week?

Week 1	_____ botos
Week 2	_____ botos
Week 3	_____ botos
Week 4	_____ botos
	Total = 80 botos

Follow the directions.

Complete the Venn diagram. Ask an adult to help you research the features of each type of dolphin. Use the words and phrases below to get you started.

| pink | gray | river | ocean |

KOKO MEETS MR. ROGERS

On July 28, 1998, a popular children's show on public television was airing an episode on inclusion of those who are different. One guest on the show had been a fan of *Mister Rogers' Neighborhood* since she was young. She herself was different and used sign language to communicate to those around her. But she wasn't a typical fan of the show. She was a gorilla.

Koko, a female western lowland gorilla, was raised by humans because she was very ill as an infant and her mother rejected her. Dr. Penny Patterson agreed to care for Koko for a few years. A few years turned into more than 40 years.

FUN FACT Koko knew more than 1,000 signs and even created some of her own new signs.

Koko was invited to be a guest on her favorite TV show. Koko removed Fred Rogers' shoes and sweater as she had seen him do every episode of the show. Fred Rogers was touched by Koko's kindness and the show became a much-loved episode by animal lovers around the world.

Several books have been written about Koko including one about her love for her kitten named "All Ball." Koko painted, came up with her own jokes, played games, and engaged in imaginative play. Koko joins Fred Rogers in the respected group of individuals who have made a positive impact on fans young and old. Individual lives matter—gorillas and humans.

Write a response to each question.

1. What pet did Koko have?
   _____

2. Name a similarity between Koko and Mr. Rogers.
   _____
   _____

3. Name a difference between Koko and Mr. Rogers.
   _____
   _____

4. Underline the sentence in the text that tells what Koko did when she met Fred Rogers. Why do you think Koko did that? Explain.
   _____
   _____
   _____

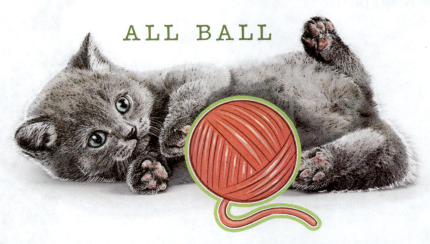

ALL BALL

Solve each problem.

1. Koko has 4 different games she wants to play. If she plays each game once a day for 4 days, how many games will she have played?

   _____ games

2. Koko loved jokes. If she told 18 jokes in 9 days, how many jokes did she tell each day?

   _____ jokes per day

3. Koko paints 3 pictures in the morning and 2 in the evening. If she paints the same number of pictures each day for one week, then how many total pictures does Koko paint?

   _____ pictures

54 UNUSUALLY FUN READING

Follow the directions.

Koko loved kittens. She had more pet kittens after All Ball. Use the sign language letters to reveal her other pet kittens' names!

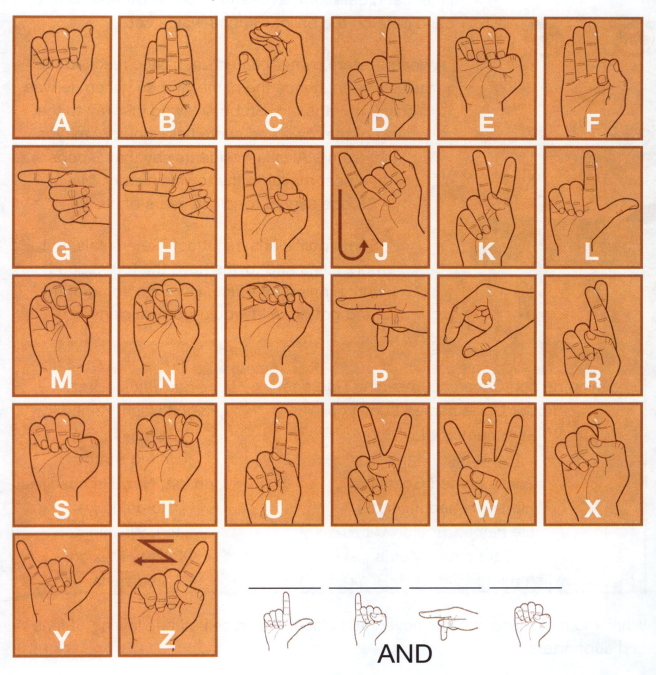

    AND

STUBBS FOR MAYOR

The story goes that a small Alaskan town did not like either candidate for mayor and wrote in Stubbs as a candidate on the ballot. Stubbs was a cat.

A general store owner named Lauri Stec rescued the tailless kitten, hence the name Stubbs, when he was only 3 months old. Stubbs clawed his way to the top of the town and served as honorary mayor. Talkeetna, Alaska, residents say that Stubbs was the best mayor in the town's history. Mayor Stubbs served for all 20 years of his life.

Some politicians might act like animals, but more cities and towns have the four-legged variety running for office. Here are some of the wild and not-so-wild would-be politicians.

*PICTURED IS ACTOR AND MAYOR STUBBS LOOK-ALIKE, CHEDDAR MEOWISE.

Animal	Where
Rhino named Cacareco (meaning *Garbage*)	Sao Paulo, Brazil
Border Collie named Lucy Lou	Rabbit Hash, Kentucky
Goat named Clay Henry	Lajitas, Texas
Pig named Pigasus	United States
Gorilla named Colossus	Hudson, New Hampshire
Horse named Incitatus	Rome, Italy
Mule named Boston Curtis	Milton, Washington
Cat named Morris	Xalapa, Mexico
Crawfish named Crawfish B. Crawfish	Louisiana

While most of these animals never held office, they received a following of fans and supporters.

FUN FACT

Animals have been observed in the wild "voting" in a majority rules decision. Honeybees for example compete to lead the rest of the bees by doing a dance-off.

Match each word to its definition.

1. candidate   over half the people or things in a group

2. hence   given as an honor without the normal requirements

3. honorary   someone who is running in an election

4. majority   for this reason

Write a response to each question.

5. What does the author mean when they say, "Some politicians might act like animals"?

_____

_____

6. Would you want an animal for mayor of your town? Why or why not?

_____

_____

_____

Use the pie chart to answer the questions.

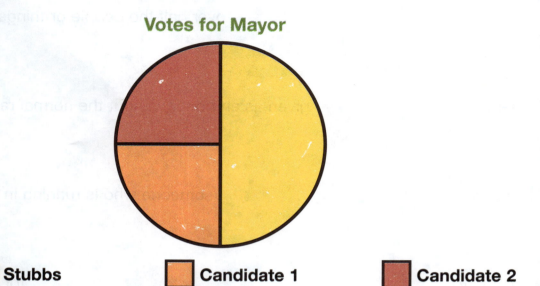

1. What fraction of votes did each candidate receive?

   Candidate 1 _____

   Candidate 2 _____

   Stubbs _____

2. Who received the most votes?

   _____

3. Which two candidates received the same number of votes?

   _____ and _____

4. What fraction of the votes do Candidate 1 and Candidate 2 make up together?

   _____

Follow the directions.

Choose one of the animal candidates (page 56). Create a campaign poster for them. Include a picture, their name, and a slogan.

BAWLING BABIES

Most of the time, the sound of a baby crying isn't what anyone wants to hear. But that's not the case for a 400-year-old Japanese ritual! Naki Sumo, or baby-cry sumo, is a festival where sumo wrestlers stand across from each other with a baby and try to make the infants cry.

FUN FACT: Although newborns are famous for their crying, you won't see any tears on their faces! Newborn babies don't develop tear ducts until a few weeks after birth.

Many of the babies don't need much encouragement because being held by a stranger in front of a crowd is enough! But for the babies slower to cry, the sumo wrestlers will shout and do their best to bring out the tears.

This tearful tradition is thought to bring good health to the babies. Each match ends with a saying, *banzai raku*, which means live long. These festivals are held at shrines across Japan where hundreds of babies and their parents gather. Some of the events even declare winners. It could be the baby to cry first or the baby to cry the loudest. Earplugs anyone!?

Complete each sentence with a word from the word bank.

| encouragement | ritual | tearful | declare |

1. A _____ is a type of ceremony.

2. A frightened baby may become _____.

3. Clapping and cheering are forms of _____.

4. To _____ a winner is to say someone's name with emphasis.

Write a response to each question.

5. What is this passage mostly about?

_____

_____

6. Would you want to attend the Naki Sumo festival? Why or why not?

_____

_____

Solve each problem.

1. There are 12 babies at the festival. If you give 3 babies to each sumo wrestler, how many sumo wrestlers are there?

   _____ sumo wrestlers

2. There are 27 babies at the festival. If you give 9 babies to each sumo wrestler, how many sumo wrestlers are there?

   _____ sumo wrestlers

Use the array to solve each problem.

3. Show one way that the babies can be divided amongst 4 sumo wrestlers.

   _____ ÷ _____ = _____ babies for each wrestler

4. Show one way that the babies can be divided between 2 sumo wrestlers.

   _____ ÷ _____ = _____ babies for each wrestler

Follow the directions.

Read all the clues in order. Color the box red if the clue does not match. Color the box green if it does match. The first box has been done for you.

Three babies were entered into the contest for loudest crier in decibels. Decide who won by matching each baby with the meter reading of his or her cry.

- Akari's cry measured an odd number of decibels.

- Mei's cry was quieter than Akari's.

- Haruto's cry measured the loudest.

	Meter 1	Meter 2	Meter 3
HARUTO			
MEI			
AKARI		(green)	

Explain your answer. _____

_____

_____

A VERY CHEESY SPORT

Have you ever dreamed of becoming a sports star? Maybe you love basketball, gymnastics, or even…cheese rolling? Head over to Gloucester, England to take part in this extreme sport!

The earliest written mention of cheese rolling dates back to 1826, but many believe it started hundreds of years before that. Contestants enter races where they chase a seven-pound wheel of cheese down Cooper's Hill to the finish line. And this is one steep hill! So steep, in fact, that contestants don't do much running in this race. You're more likely to see these racers rolling down the hill after the cheese. Rugby players wait at the bottom of the hill to help catch people as they come down.

SAY CHEESE!

FUN FACT Cheese has been around a long time. Longer than any written language!

WINNER
TRUE LOVE

The idea is to catch the cheese, but the cheese goes way too fast for that! It can reach speeds up to 70 mph (113 kph), so the winner is the one who makes it to the finish first. You may have already guessed what prize winners are taking home. They get to walk away with the wheel of cheese they chased to the bottom!

64 UNUSUALLY FUN READING & MATH GRADE 3

Write the meaning of each word.

1. contestant: _____

_____

2. extreme: _____

_____

3. language: _____

_____

4. rugby: _____

_____

Write a response to each question.

5. Why do you think people compete in cheese rolling races?

_____

_____

_____

6. How is the winner declared? What do they win?

_____

_____

_____

Solve the multiplication facts in each wheel.

Example:

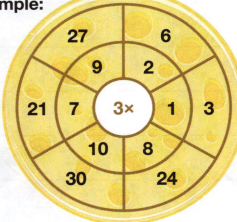

1.

2.

3.
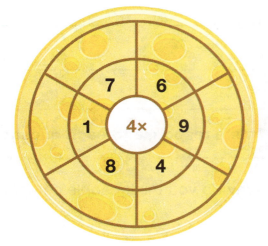

4.
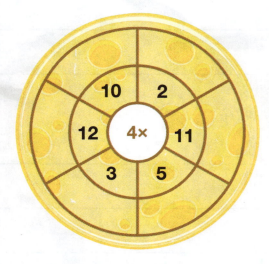

5.
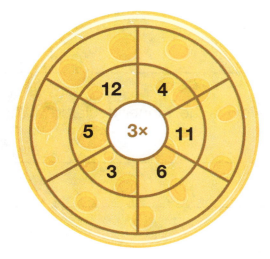

66 UNUSUALLY FUN READING & MATH GRADE 3

Find the names of 10 different types of cheese.

BLUE CHEESE   MOZZARELLA
BRIE   PARMESAN
CHEDDAR   PEPPER JACK
COTTAGE CHEESE QUESO BLANCO
FETA   RICOTTA

```
Q U E S O B L A N C O P O A
J O Q D R L N J V P N A U M
R M O Z Z A R E L L A R A F
I P B V B N Q G G Z E M V P
C T M L A E G T M T S E C F
O U W K U Y V E G P P S R M
T Z D L P E P P E R J A C K
T D U U J S C D U X E N N Q
A Z A U P R I H W C A G N N
D M X T J Q H Q E H X O U U
C O T T A G E C H E E S E V
B O W G F J B M L D S L Q X
U R D I G N W X M D T E T B
B Z I B P Z T Y A A R F I P
F W D E F E T A K R R I R M
```

DINING ON DOG FOOD

Eating dog food may not be something you'd consider doing on your average day. But for pet food testers, that's just part of the job! These dogged professionals make sure your pets are eating the very best.

Eating the food isn't the only part of the job. It also requires plenty of research and creativity, as these workers are also often tasked with creating new recipes.

When it comes time to test the product, one of the key aspects is making sure the food is nutritious. Then the tester will evaluate the smell. Part of a dog's interest in food comes from the smell. Not only that but if food is too smelly, pet owners won't want it in their homes!

Finally, the taste test. Testers will taste for flavor and texture. If they think it's gross, it's likely the dog will too! When they've made their judgements, they spit out the food. Probably a good way to avoid any stomach aches!

FUN FACT — A dog's sense of smell can be up to 1,000 times better than a human's. Dogs have been known to smell their owners from as far away as 18 miles (29 km)!

Match each word to its definition.

1. texture   how something tastes

2. judgment   the feel and appearance of something

3. nutritious   an opinion or decision

4. flavor   providing nutrients

Write a response to each question.

5. What four factors do dog food testers take into consideration when testing the food?

_____   _____

_____   _____

6. Would you want to be a dog food tester? Explain.

Solve each problem. Draw food in the bowls to show the answers.

1.

2.

3.

4.

Solve each problem.

5. One small bag of food will feed a dog for one week. If the dog eats twice a day, how many meals are in each bag?

   _____ meals

6. One large bag of food will feed a dog for one month (assume 30 days). If the dog eats twice a day, how many meals are in each bag?

   _____ meals

Follow the directions.

Your boss asks you to shorten this recipe to fit on a small pet food label. Write the fraction for each part of the ingredient.

BUT, BOSS! I CAN'T EVEN HOLD A PENCIL!

Maggie's Meaty Meals

One-half of a pound of ground turkey	_____ lb. of ground turkey
One and one-fourth teaspoons of oil	_____ tsp. oil
Three and one-half cups of water	_____ cups water
Three-fourths cup of brown rice	_____ cup brown rice
Two-thirds cup of split peas	_____ cup split peas
One and one-half tablespoons of broth	_____ tbsp. broth
One-third cup of carrots	_____ cup carrots

HAMBURGER HARRY

Would you ever want to be surrounded by your favorite food? The home of Harry Sperl, also known as Hamburger Harry, is filled to the brim with burgers! Harry is the world record holder for largest hamburger collection. When he was declared a world record holder, he had 3,724 hamburger related items.

His hamburger collection began accidentally. He was searching for a fake burger that he could use in a photograph and ended up buying five options. When a coworker saw all the burgers on his desk, he asked Harry if he was collecting them. He thought, well maybe now I should!

FUN FACT

The most expensive burger ever sold went for $5,964! The chef created the pricey burger so that he could donate the money to charity. It included ingredients like caviar, crab, and white truffle.

In over 26 years of collecting, Harry's collection has grown significantly from those few fake burgers. Now he has tons of hamburger toys, hamburger accessories, and even a hamburger motorcycle! Harry made the motorcycle himself, and he loves driving around his town showing off his creation, hamburger helmet and all!

Write a sentence for each word from the passage.

1. creation: _____

_____

2. brim: _____

_____

3. collection: _____

_____

4. options: _____

_____

Write a response to each question.

5. Harry's hamburger collection started by accident. How do you think he feels about this? Support your answer with evidence from the text.

_____

_____

_____

6. If you were going to start a collection of something, what would you collect? Why would you choose this item?

_____

_____

Use the data to make a bar graph. Round each number to the nearest ten.

Hamburger Collectibles

🍔	Plushies	25
🏷️	Artwork	68
👜	Accessories	37
🔑	Keychains	61
🍔	Figurines	84

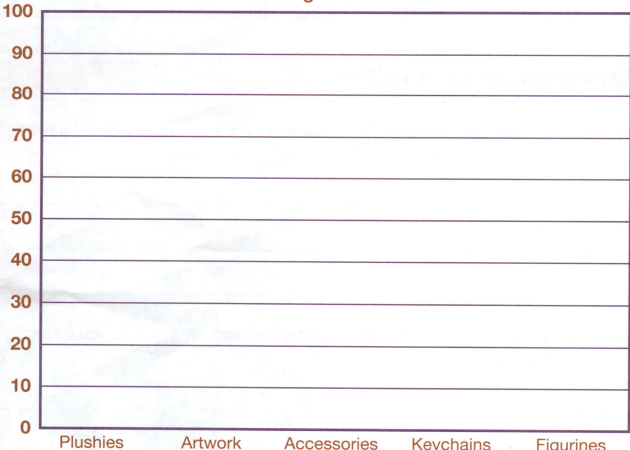

Hamburger Collectibles

Follow the directions.

Find your way through the ketchup maze! On the lines, write the letters you pass through in order to spell out one of Harry's largest collectibles.

_____

CELEBRATING SOCKS

Why is it so tricky to keep a pair of socks together? The case of the missing sock seems to be a problem that many people experience. A study conducted in Great Britain found that the average person loses 1.3 socks each month, which means more than 15 socks a year! Where do those pesky socks walk off to?

While we may never conquer our sock loss conundrum, we sure can celebrate it! That's where Lost Sock Memorial Day comes in. Every May 9th, you can honor your lost socks with this silly day of recognition.

How might you celebrate this wacky holiday? You could get creative and use one of your lone socks to make a sock puppet. You could also ask a parent if you can donate some socks to an organization that helps people experiencing homelessness.

THE USUAL SUSPECT

FUN FACT — Historians think the first socks date back to the Stone Age and were made from animal skins that were tied around a person's ankle.

Answer each question.

1. Which of the following is a synonym for *pesky*?

   A. happy

   B. lost

   C. naughty

2. Which of the following is a synonym for *honor*?

   A. insult

   B. remember

   C. forget

Write a response to each question.

3. What is the problem in this passage?

   _____

   _____

   _____

4. Besides making a sock puppet, list three things that you could do with a sock that is missing its mate.

   _____

   _____

   _____

Solve each problem.

1. How many socks does the Miller family lose in a year if they lose 3 socks per month?

   _____ socks

2. How many socks does the Lopez family lose in a year if they lose 2 socks per month?

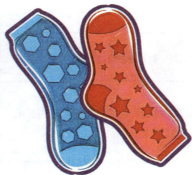

   _____ socks

3. How many socks does the Stein family lose in a year if they lose 4 socks per month?

   _____ socks

Follow the directions.

Your sock drawer has spilled. One sock has no mate. Find it. Then, write a description of what it looks like.

_____

_____

WACKY LAWS

While some laws are made to keep us safe and protected, you can find plenty that don't make any sense! In these cases, you can't help but wonder, what happened that made them put this law in place?

That's especially the case with a law in Alabama. This law states that it is illegal to wear a fake mustache to church if it causes laughter. Better leave your costumes at home folks.

If you're a big fan of silly string you better stay out of Mobile, Alabama. It's illegal to buy, sell, or use silly string there!

In Kansas, eating cherry pie is serious business. So serious, that at one point it was illegal to put ice cream on cherry pie. It's unclear how this one became a law or if it is still in place, but don't worry, this one isn't enforced!

FAKE MUSTACHE

SILLY STRING

ICE CREAM ON CHERRY PIE

FUN FACT

Silly string isn't the only celebratory substance outlawed in Mobile, Alabama. Confetti is also illegal there!

Write the definition of each word. Use the word in a sentence.

1. illegal:

_____

_____

2. enforced:

_____

_____

Write a response to each question.

3. What are three silly things in Alabama that people could get in trouble for doing?

_____

_____

_____

4. Why do you think some of these laws were written?

_____

_____

_____

Use the table to write a ticket for each offender.

Law Broken	Fine
A. Using a can of silly string	$1,000
B. Chewing gum in public	$650
C. Wearing a fake mustache	$225
D. Flicking boogers into the wind	$150
E. Carrying an ice cream cone in a pocket	$450

1. Sam broke laws **B** and **D**.

   TICKET NO. 000001
   NOTICE OF VIOLATION

   FINE: _____

2. Liv broke laws **C** and **E**.

   TICKET NO. 000002
   NOTICE OF VIOLATION

   FINE: _____

3. Gabe broke laws **A**, **C**, and **E**.

   TICKET NO. 000003
   NOTICE OF VIOLATION

   FINE: _____

Follow the directions.

Make up your own wacky law. Complete the sentence below. Then, draw a comic strip showing an event where the law is broken.

In the state of _____ it is illegal to _____

_____

when you are _____.

UNUSUALLY FUN READING & MATH GRADE 3

SLEEPING ON THE JOB

You may have heard that it is not a good idea to fall asleep at work or at school. But what if sleeping on the job really is your job? Sounds like a dream!

Professional sleepers are hired for several different industries. Hotels hire people to test out the comfort levels of mattresses, lighting, and noise. Makers of sleep-enhancing products and medicines hire professional sleepers to test products.

Good professional sleepers need to have certain skills, and not just being a sound sleeper. They must be in good health and must be able to sleep in new surroundings. They must have good observational skills and be able to write detailed reports.

FUN FACT Scientists who study sleep found out that most people sleep on their sides.

If a Professional Sleeper sounds like your dream job, then you'd better get started training. Your bedtime is approaching. Zzzzzzz…

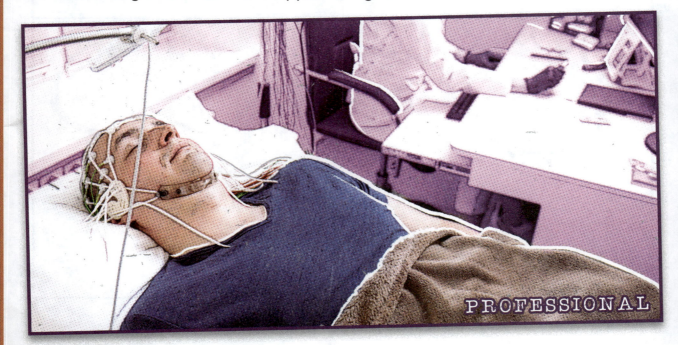

Write an antonym for each word.

1. asleep: _____

2. dream: _____

3. hire: _____

Answer each question.

4. Which of these statements tell what the passage is mostly about?

    A. Sleeping is fun.

    B. Sleeping can be a job.

    C. Sleep is part of a healthy lifestyle.

5. Which of the following are necessary skills for a professional sleeper?

    A. Good at math and science

    B. Sound sleeper and good eater

    C. Healthy and able to write detailed reports

UNUSUALLY FUN READING & MATH GRADE 3   85

Solve for *n* in each problem.

1. Mike sleeps for 7 hours a day. His goal is to sleep for 49 hours that week. After 5 days, how many hours does Mike have left to sleep to meet his goal?

   7 × 5 + n = 49

   _____ hours

2. Zuri sleeps for 8 hours a day. Her goal is to sleep for 56 hours that week. After 4 days, how many hours does Zuri have left to sleep to meet her goal?

   8 × 4 + n = 56

   _____ hours

Solve the problem.

3. Daxton is trying to earn $120 sleeping at the hotel. He has earned $80 so far. If he makes $5 an hour, how many hours does he need to sleep to reach his goal?

   _____ hours

86

Follow the directions.

Write the missing numbers in each pillow puzzle. The sum of each row, column, and diagonal must be 15. The first one has been done for you.

BEACHCOMBING FOR TOYS

Going boldly where no explorer has gone before, a little yellow rubber ducky is the subject of a quack-y story involving a cargo ship, ocean tides, and some curious beachcombers.

Beachcombing is a hobby where people "comb" beaches looking for interesting things. Finding little yellow plastic ducks washed ashore amongst shells and rocks made some beachcombers wonder where they came from. An offshore event in 1992 would explain everything.

A large shipping container holding 28,800 plastic bath toys fell from a cargo ship in the Pacific Ocean. The ship departed Hong Kong and was headed to Tacoma, Washington. A weather report later revealed that there was rough weather during the ship's voyage.

FUN FACT: In addition to plastic bath toys, beachcombers have found name-brand sneakers and popular interlocking blocks. Funny enough, the blocks included ocean-themed pieces such as octopuses, sharks, diving flippers, life rafts, and more!

The ducks, along with other bath toys from the container, ended up on the coasts of Alaska and even further north. After a 15-year journey, some of the toys were found in Europe. Some may still be drifting around the globe. Beachcombers be on the lookout! There could be little yellow duckies washing ashore at a beach near you!

Write a sentence for each word. Use the part of speech given.

1. voyage (n): _____

2. rough (adj): _____

3. drifting (v): _____

Write a response to each question.

4. What most likely caused the container to fall off the ship?

_____

_____

5. How would this story be different if the container had been filled with heavy items like bricks and metal?

_____

_____

_____

_____

THE GREAT ESCAPE!

For each object, circle the appropriate unit of measurement.

1. The weight of a shipping container

   grams   pounds   tons

2. The weight of a rubber duck

   grams   pounds   tons

3. The weight of a person beachcombing

   grams   pounds   tons

Round each weight to the nearest hundred.

4. 345 pounds

   _____

5. 476 grams

   _____

6. 198 tons

   _____

7. 813 pounds

   _____

WELL THIS EXPLAINS HOW WE FALL OFF.

Follow the directions.

Look at the map below. Measure the approximate distance each duck traveled from the ship in inches. Use the key to complete the table.

Distance Traveled	
Duck A	_____ miles
Duck B	_____ miles
Duck C	_____ miles
Duck D	_____ miles

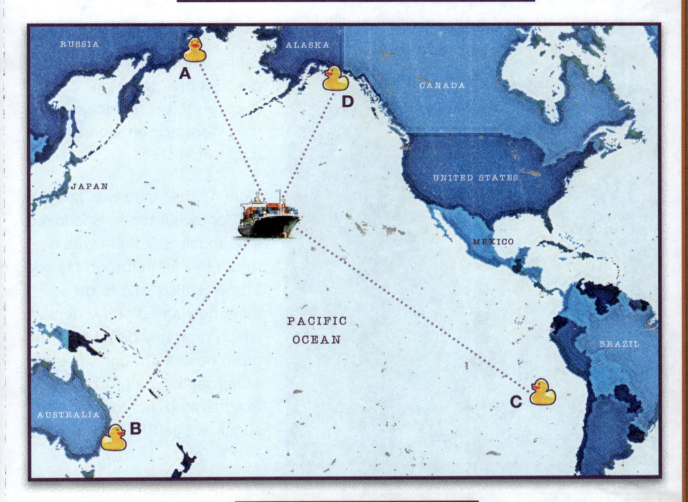

one-half inch = 1,000 miles

ROTTEN TEETH

Sugar wasn't always easy for the average person to get their hands on. Back in Tudor England it was pricey. Sugar had to be brought in from places such as New Guinea.

This meant that only wealthy people indulged in sugary treats. Because it was the rich who could afford sugary food, it was also the rich who showed higher signs of tooth decay. Rotting teeth became a sign of great wealth!

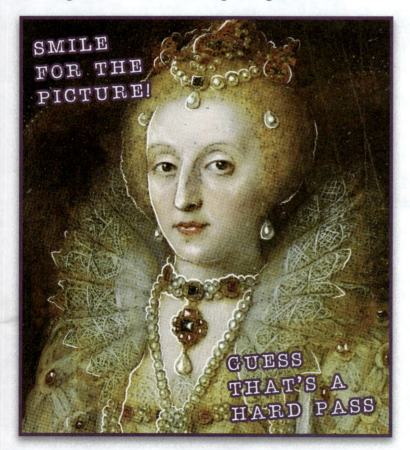

SMILE FOR THE PICTURE!

GUESS THAT'S A HARD PASS

Some went as far as to blacken their teeth on purpose to make it look as if they were rich enough to have a sugary diet.

Queen Elizabeth I was famous for her sweet tooth. She loved it so much that there was a rumor her teeth turned black! She was also said to be extremely afraid of the dentist, which probably didn't help her tooth health. Though the state of her teeth was probably exaggerated, her love of sugar was not!

FUN FACT — Sugar was even used as medicine. People thought it helped with digestion.

Complete each sentence with a word from the word bank.

rumor	rare	digestion

1. Sugar was once so expensive, it was considered _____ for poorer people to have any.

2. There was a _____ that Queen Elizabeth's teeth turned black because she ate so much sugar.

3. People thought that sugar helped with _____, so they treated it like a medicine.

Write a response to each question.

4. What is the main idea of the text?

_____

_____

_____

5. What is one way sugar was used in the past that is different from today's uses?

_____

_____

_____

SO WORTH IT

Use the table to answer each question.

Royal Family Member	Number of Rotten Teeth
Queen Elizabeth	ⲐⲐⲐⲐ Ⲓ
King Henry	ⲐⲐⲐⲐ ⲐⲐⲐ
Earl of Manchester	ⲐⲐ
Princess Victoria	ⲐⲐⲐⲐ

1. Which royal had the most rotten teeth?

   _____

2. Which royal had the least rotten teeth?

   _____

3. Create a pictograph showing the data.

Royal Family Member	Number of Rotten Teeth
Queen Elizabeth	
King Henry	
Earl of Manchester	
Princess Victoria	

= 1 rotten tooth

Follow the directions.

Make these teeth rotten! Figure out the counting pattern. Color the teeth black that do not fit the pattern. Write the correct numbers for the pattern.

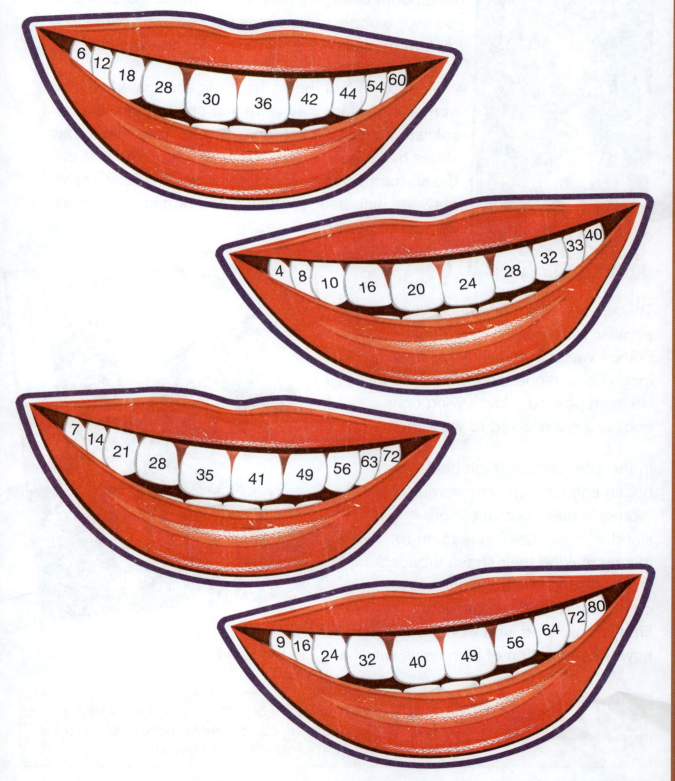

HIGH HEEL HISTORY

Fashion is often gender-specific, meaning some trends are thought of as feminine and some as masculine. Have you ever wondered how these stereotypes came to be? Look to the history of high heels for an example!

While today's high heels are most associated with women's fashion, they were first created for Persian soldiers in the 10th century. They realized that if their shoes had a heel, it was easier to keep their feet in the stirrups when they rode a horse. The relationship between high heels, soldiers, and horses made heels a symbol of power and wealth.

THE P.O.
(Persian Original)

This association made heels very popular with nobility. King Louis XIV of France was a particularly big fan! He made heels higher and more colorful. He even passed a law saying only nobility were allowed to wear them.

In the 18th century, high heels began catching on with women. Women's heels became more slender. Men's fashion reacted to this by making their shoes broader. By the 1730s, the transition was complete. High heels became firmly associated with women. But who knows how the reputation of high heels will change in the future!

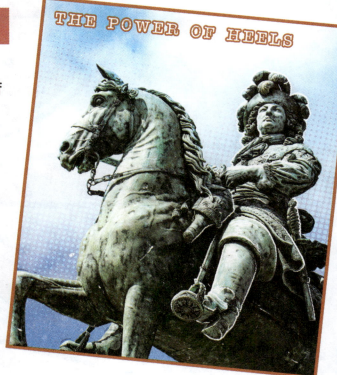

THE POWER OF HEELS

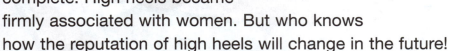

FUN FACT — Cowboy boots, which are often worn by ranchers, can be traced directly back to the 10th century Persian heels!

Write a synonym for each word.

1. slender: _____

2. wealthy: _____

3. popular: _____

4. colorful: _____

Put these events in the order that they happened.

5. _____ Women's shoes became slender, and men's shoes became wider.

_____ High heels became strictly known as a feminine shoe.

_____ People of nobility started wearing high heels.

_____ King Louis XIV passed a law that only people of nobility could wear high heels.

_____ High heels were created for Persian soldiers.

Complete the sentence with your own words.

6. It would be almost impossible to _____,

_____, or _____

while wearing high heels.

Use the pictures to answer each question.

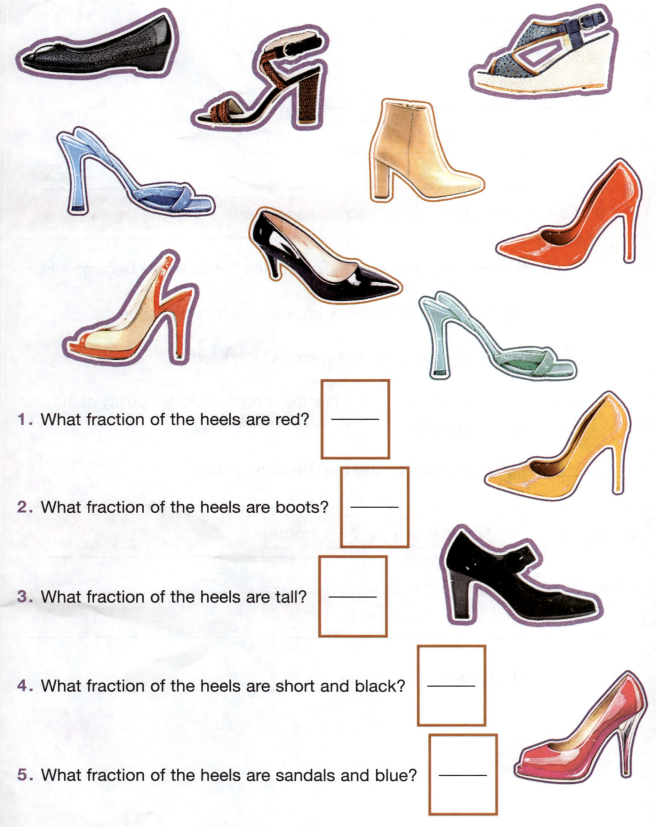

1. What fraction of the heels are red? _____

2. What fraction of the heels are boots? _____

3. What fraction of the heels are tall? _____

4. What fraction of the heels are short and black? _____

5. What fraction of the heels are sandals and blue? _____

Follow the directions.

Draw the missing heels so that each heel appears only once in each row, column, or square.

SNIFF THIS!

If you think you've got a good sense of smell, you can use your talents to make some money! From the silly sounding to the very serious, professional sniffers can have a wide variety of jobs.

Armpit sniffers put their talents to the test through, you guessed it, sniffing armpits. Companies testing out new products that try to get rid of body odor need a way to determine which one works best. That's where the sniffing comes in. After the test subjects work up a sweat wearing a new deodorant, the armpit sniffer will smell their armpits to see how effective the deodorant was!

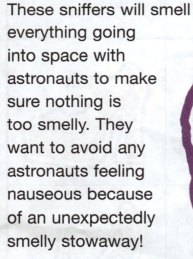

GOTCH'R NOSE!

Professional sniffers aren't just used for detecting body odor. NASA needs them too! They have an entire team dedicated to odor. These sniffers will smell everything going into space with astronauts to make sure nothing is too smelly. They want to avoid any astronauts feeling nauseous because of an unexpectedly smelly stowaway!

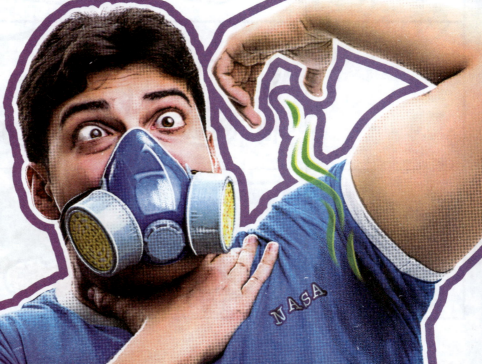

FUN FACT

Researchers have found that two percent of people have armpits that don't smell!

100

Use each word in a sentence.

1. detect: _____

2. nauseous: _____

3. rid: _____

4. talent: _____

Write a response to each question.

5. How do you think the author feels about professional sniffers? How do you know? Use details from the passage to support your answer.

_____

_____

_____

_____

6. List four things that could be too smelly to send into space with astronauts.

_____

_____

_____

_____

Solve each problem.

The Corner Store		
Deodorants	Price	50% off Heat Wave Sale
Stinky No More	$4.00	
Smell Like a Rose	$5.00	
Sweat Blaster	$2.00	
P U Spray	$7.00	
Fresh Pits	$3.00	
Armpit Flower Power	$6.00	

1. If your mom sent you to The Corner Store with $12, which deodorants could you buy so that you spend all of the money? List three combinations.

_____

_____

_____

2. When there is a heat wave, the store sells their deodorants at 50% off. Write the discounted price of each deodorant in the table above.

3. Complete the table below.

Professional Armpit Smeller	Per Armpit Charge ($)	Number of Armpits Smelled	Amount Earned ($)
Lacy	$7		$49
Renaldo	$25	3	
Liu	$15	6	
Tan		4	$40
Emmett	$20		$100

4. Who made the most money? _____

5. Who made the least money? _____

Follow the directions.

Circle the best unit of length for each problem. To solve the riddle, write each circled letter in order on the lines.

Question: What did one eye say to the other?

1. Length of a car

    A. centimeters

    O. meters

2. Length of a caterpillar

    T. centimeters

    S. meters

3. Width of a bedroom

    H. meters

    N. kilometers

4. Length of a strawberry

    N. centimeters

    T. meters

5. Length of a pencil

    S. inches

    O. feet

6. Height of a giraffe

    L. inches

    M. feet

7. Length of a bed

    B. inches

    L. feet

8. Height of a skyscraper

    S. meters

    L. centimeters

Answer: Between you and me,

S ____ ME ____ ____ I ____ G

____ ____ E ____ L ____ !

UNUSUALLY FUN READING & MATH GRADE 3

TOOTHY TRADITIONS

Losing a baby tooth is a special moment. But not everyone celebrates this milestone the same way! You might be familiar with the Tooth Fairy who is popular in North America. But she wasn't the first of the magical tooth collectors. In fact, her story came about through a mix of different legends. One of those being the legend of a little tooth-collecting mouse.

This little mouse is well known in many Spanish-speaking countries such as Spain and Mexico. Ratoncito, or *El Raton de Los Dientes* (the tooth mouse), became known as a collector of teeth. Much like the Tooth Fairy, this mouse visits children who lose a tooth and leaves them a present or money in its place.

FUN FACT

Ratoncito Pérez has his own museum in Madrid, Spain. Visitors can learn about the mouse and even see baby teeth from famous people such as Isaac Newton and Beatrix Potter.

Some people don't just leave baby teeth lying around for friendly creatures to find. In some Asian countries, children go outside and toss their teeth to the sky or throw them onto a roof. Many will toss their lower teeth up and their upper teeth down, sometimes burying the upper teeth. This symbolizes the wish for their teeth to grow in the right direction.

PAY DAY!

Match each word to its meaning.

1. legend — an action or event marking a significant development

2. moment — a person who collects things

3. milestone — a traditional story

4. collector — a brief period in time

Write a response to each question.

5. Does everyone celebrate losing a tooth the same way? How do you know?
_____
_____
_____

6. Why do you think losing teeth is celebrated in many cultures?
_____
_____

7. How do you celebrate losing your teeth? _____
_____

UNUSUALLY FUN READING & MATH GRADE 3

Solve each problem.

1. Most babies are born with 20 teeth hidden under their gums. Adults have 32 teeth. How many more teeth do adults have than babies?

   _____ teeth

2. Mrs. Tanner had a set of triplets. They were born with 48 teeth in all. How many teeth was each baby born with?

   _____ teeth

Answer each question.

3. Complete the table below to show how many teeth Ratoncito has collected in one month. (He takes weekends off!)

	Monday	Tuesday	Wednesday	Thursday	Friday	TOTAL
Week 1	15	12	6		8	45
Week 2		11	7	8	6	37
Week 3	16	9	14	5	8	
Week 4	5	3		18	12	40

4. Which week did Ratoncito collect the most teeth? _____

5. How many teeth did Ratoncito collect in one month?

   _____ teeth

Follow the directions.

Help the Tooth Fairy find the tooth. Follow the path with correct comparisons.

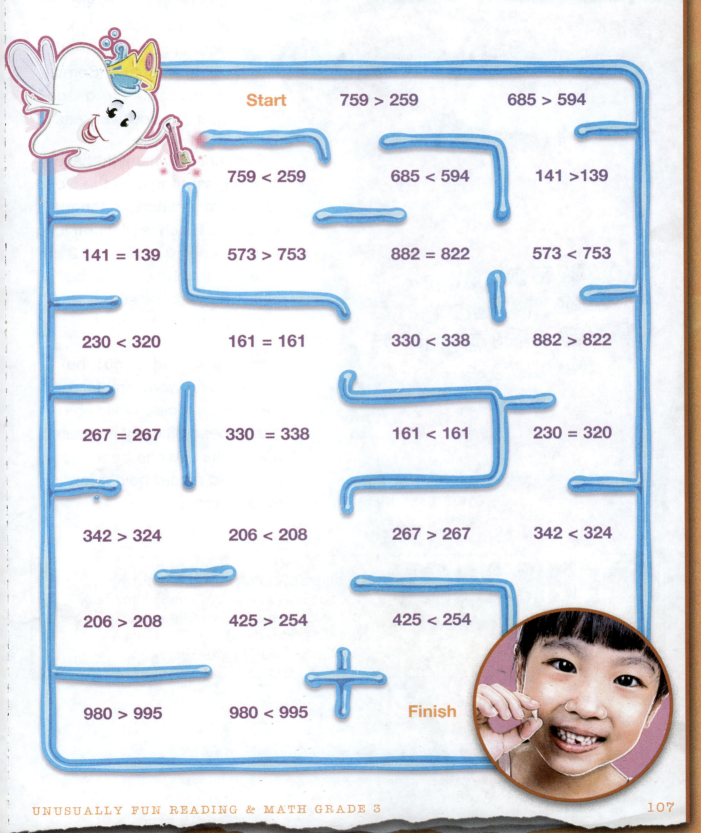

TONGUE TWISTED

Maybe you've heard it's impossible to lick your elbow. Well, that's not exactly true. Some people can! For Adrianne Lewis, it's positively easy.

Adrianne Lewis might have the longest tongue in the world. The average woman's tongue is around 3.1 inches (7.9 cm) long. Adrianne's is 4 inches (10.2 cm)! She can touch her nose, her chin, and yes, her elbow. She can even touch her eye!

Adrianne started a YouTube channel and went viral for her tongue tricks. While she hasn't been officially measured, she thinks she can beat the world record holder for longest tongue.

WHAT DO YOU CALL TONGUES THAT ARE BEST FRIENDS?

TASTE BUDS!

FUN FACT

In different cultures, sticking out your tongue has different meanings. In some places, like the United States, it's considered rude. But in Tibet, it's a customary way to greet someone!

Write the meaning of each word as it is used in the text.

1. viral: _____

2. rude: _____

Write a response to each question.

3. Why is it easy for Adrianne to touch parts of her face with her tongue? Use evidence from the text to support your answer.

   _____

   _____

4. Would you like to have a longer tongue? Explain.

   _____

   _____

UNUSUALLY FUN READING & MATH GRADE 3

Use the diagram to answer each question.

1. How much longer is Lynne's leg than her arm?

   _____ in.

2. How much shorter is Lynne's torso than her leg?

   _____ in.

3. Which is longer, Lynne's head or her hand? _____

Lynne

top of head to bottom of head: 12 in.

hand: 8 in.

arm: 30 in.

torso: 24 in.

leg: 36 in.

Follow the directions.

Use a measuring tape to measure five different parts of your body. Label the parts. Write the measurements.

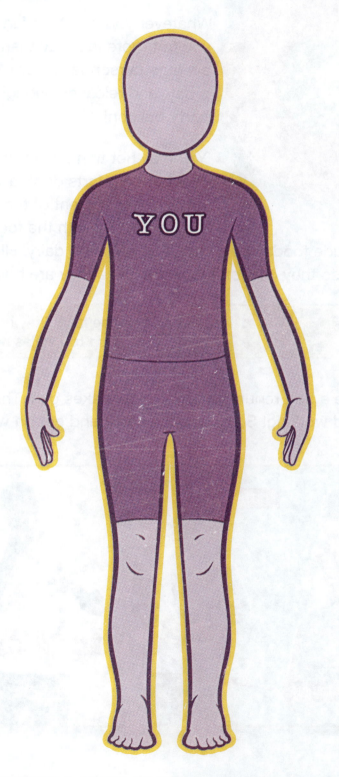

GASSY FACTS

Pffft...What was that? Was it you!? Probably.

Whatever you call it—a fart, fizzler, or toot—you fart more in a day than you think! The average person farts from 10 to 20 times a day, and releases enough gas to fill a party balloon!

You may not think you fart this much because most of your farts don't actually smell. Only around one percent of them will smell foul. It all has to do with the food you ate. The smelly culprits include foods like beans, broccoli, and dairy. High-fiber foods take longer to process, so they give off more gas while they are being digested.

FUN FACT Farts can be fast! They have been measured at speeds up to 7 miles per hour.

Although farts have a bad reputation, everyone makes gas. They're a sign your body is healthy and working! So, excuse yourself and get on with your day.

Complete each sentence with a word from the word bank.

| average | culprits | reputation |

1. Although farts are a sign of a healthy digestive system, they have a bad _____.

2. The _____ person farts enough gas to fill a party balloon.

3. Smelly _____ such as broccoli and beans can cause stinky farts.

Answer each question.

4. What is the author's purpose for writing this passage?

   A. To inform you about farts.

   B. To persuade you that farts do not smell.

   C. To entertain you.

   D. Both A. and C.

5. What does the author say farts are a sign of?

   A. Your body is healthy and working.

   B. You have bad manners.

   C. They are the best way to blow up balloons.

UNUSUALLY FUN READING & MATH GRADE 3   113

Use the data in the table to answer each question.

Simmons Family	Average Number of Farts Per Day
Lorena	10
Robby	19
Maxton	9
Carley	15
Mom	10
Dad	17
Hoover (the dog)	30

1. How many more farts does Hoover the dog have than Mom?

    two times as many   three times as many

2. Which two children together have as many farts as Robby?

   _____

Create two word problems using the data in the table. Solve each problem.

3. _____

   _____

4. _____

   _____

114   UNUSUALLY FU...   MATH GRADE 3

Find 10 different words and phrases for a fart in the puzzle.

TOOT	PASS GAS
POOT	CUT THE CHEESE
FIZZLER	FLATULENCE
FLOOF	ZINGER
BREAK WIND	STEP ON A FROG

```
T Q W N U U Q B U T E C F X G
F O V X A R N R S O M V C B O
N B O A B Y E R E O U U X S R
A J X T F R E G U P T L E B F
O A D Q G L E P N T H W H L A
P R I G Z N L A H I A D X P N
V M C Z B Y Z E K D Z N C A O
Q N I Y Y Z C S L W S S G S P
H F Z C X H B C M O I R S S E
C N S N E F L O O F I N V G T
E C N E L U T A L F M A D A S
J Z S K F M F C I Z S V Y S M
F E P Y B N P C V L A C P T Z
```

GROWING IN SPACE

Earth's gravity is making you shorter! If you want to add a couple inches to your height, try becoming an astronaut. In space, astronauts can grow up to three percent taller without Earth's gravity pulling them down.

In space, the backbone of an astronaut can relax and expand. This makes astronauts taller. You're probably wondering what happens when these astronauts return to Earth. Back under the pressure of gravity, they'll return to their original height.

Not only will astronauts go back to their normal height, but many will experience back pain too. That's also due to gravity! Muscles don't have to do as much work to hold you up in space. Now scientists are working on exercises to help fix the problem when astronauts return to Earth.

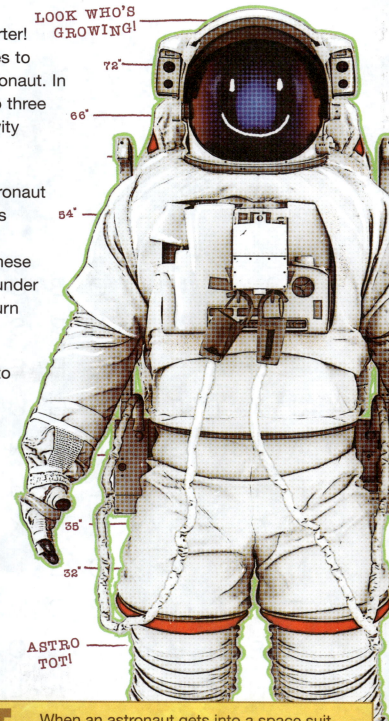

LOOK WHO'S GROWING!
72"
66"
54"
35"
32"
ASTRO TOT!

FUN FACT

When an astronaut gets into a space suit, they'll often have to be in it for five to eight hours straight! How do they go to the bathroom? Easy, they wear diapers!

Match each word to its definition.

1. relax   to become loose, less tense

2. expand   the force made by pressing against something

3. pressure   to become larger or longer

Write a response to each question.

4. How does gravity affect astronauts when they return to Earth?

_____

_____

5. What are scientists now working on to help astronauts?

_____

_____

Solve each problem.

1. Convert the astronauts' heights into inches.

5 ft. 10 inches =　　　6 ft. 1 inch =　　　6 ft. =　　　5 ft. 6 inches =

_____ inches　　_____ inches　　_____ inches　　_____ inches

2. When Alvina blasted off into space, she was 5 feet 8 inches tall. When she returned to earth, she was 5 feet 11 inches tall. How many inches did she grow when she was in space?

_____ inches

Answer the question.

3. Astronauts Adam and Alex have a height difference of 7 inches. Will this difference in height change when they are in space? Explain your answer using numbers, words, and/or pictures.

Follow the directions.

Read all the clues in order. Color the box red if the clue does not match. Color the box green if it does match. The first box has been done for you.

Three astronauts flew into space. Determine which astronaut wore their space suit for the longest amount of time.

- Adam put on his space suit in the morning.

- Alvina had her space suit on for the shortest time.

- Alex wore his space suit in the afternoon.

	1:30 p.m.–5:15 p.m.	8:00 a.m.–1:45 p.m.	3:30 p.m.–11:30 p.m.
ALVINA _____ hours _____ minutes			
ALEX _____ hours _____ minutes			
ADAM _____ hours _____ minutes		(green)	

Explain your answer. _____

TURNING ORANGE

Maybe you've heard the saying, "You are what you eat." In the case of carrots, that can be sort of true. Eat too many carrots and you may turn orange!

It's not just carrots; any food that has a high amount of a color called beta-carotene can do it. If you find your diet filled with carrots, cantaloupe, squash, and sweet potatoes, keep an eye out. You may notice a skin color change!

If your skin does turn orange, you probably developed the condition called *carotenemia*. Don't worry, it's not dangerous. You must mix up your diet to make it go away! Your skin should return to normal in a few months.

WELL, ORANGE YOU HAPPY!

FUN FACT

While eating enough carrots to turn your skin orange may seem far-fetched, the condition happens often with babies! Baby food like pureed carrots and sweet potatoes are usually the culprit.

CARROTS

SWEET POTATOES

SQUASH

ORANGES

CANTALOUPE

Write a response to each question.

1. Make a list of foods from the text that might cause you to turn orange if you eat too much of them. Ask an adult to help you research more foods to add to your list.

_____   _____

_____   _____

2. How do you make carotenemia go away?

_____

_____

3. What do you think the author means by the phrase *mix up your diet*?

_____

_____

4. What food could you eat A LOT of? What might happen to your body if you eat too much of it? Draw a picture and write a paragraph.

Use the data to complete the table.

1. Ollie noticed his skin turning orange. His mom told him to keep track of what he was eating.

   - On Monday he ate 7 slices of cantaloupe, 4 sweet potatoes, 13 carrots.
   - On Tuesday he ate 12 slices of cantaloupe, 6 sweet potatoes, 12 carrots.
   - On Wednesday he ate 9 slices of cantaloupe, 3 sweet potatoes, 14 carrots.

Day	Cantaloupe	Sweet Potatoes	Carrots
Monday			
Tuesday			
Wednesday			
TOTAL			

2. What food did Ollie eat the most of? _____

3. What food did Ollie eat the least of? _____

4. If Ollie ate 10 more carrots on Thursday and each bag of carrots has 12 carrots in it, how many bags of carrots did he open in all?

_____ bags

Write the value of each food item.

OH YOU DID NOT JUST CALL ME A YAM!

AMAZING EARWAX

What's that gunk inside your ears all about? While earwax may seem gross, it is also very useful. Much like tears in your eyes, earwax keeps your ears moisturized. That helps make sure your ears don't get itchy. Earwax will also clean itself out of your ears! No cleaning by you required. Pretty useful stuff!

Earwax has a funny relationship with sweat. Have you ever noticed that you sweat more if you're scared? The same thing is happening inside your ears! Fear can make your ears increase earwax production.

HEY, IS THERE ANY EARWAX DOWN THERE?

FUN FACT

A whale's earwax can teach a scientist a lot! Whales develop long earwax plugs that scientists can cut into and figure out how old the whale is.

YUCK!

GROSS!

EEEEEEWWW!

Earwax can also tell you if you should be worried about getting smelly when you sweat. If your earwax looks white and flaky, you probably also don't have much body odor. But if your earwax is dark and sticky, you're probably on the smelly side! Don't worry, both are normal.

Read the words from the text. Write another form of each word.

Example: happening ___happen___

1. production _____

2. relationship _____

3. moisturized _____

Write a response to each question.

4. Why does the author say that earwax is *pretty useful stuff*?

_____
_____
_____

5. What surprised you most about this passage? Explain.

_____
_____
_____

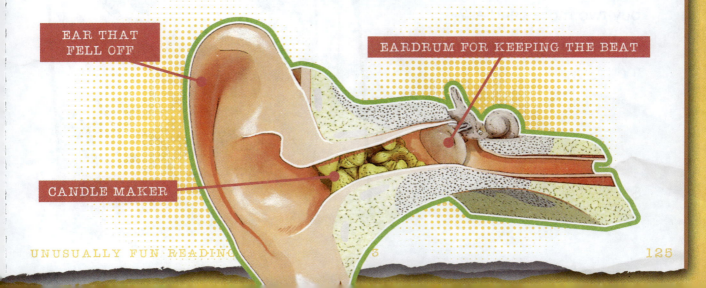

UNUSUALLY FUN READING 125

Solve each problem.

1. Ellie has too much earwax. She is going to ride her bike to the store to buy earwax drops. Her mom gave her $10. If the drops cost $7.50 after tax, how much change will Ellie get back?

    $ _____

2. With the change that Ellie gets back, how many $0.50 candies can she buy?

    _____ candies

3. Ellie's dad sends her back to the store with enough money to buy him two bottles of earwax drops. How much did her dad give her if she had only enough change to buy two more candies?

    $ _____

Follow the directions.

Draw four more globs of earwax in the squares. No glob should be in the same line (either horizontal, vertical, or diagonal) as another glob.

BABY BONES

Who has more bones, babies or adults? Believe it or not, the answer is babies! Despite being much smaller, when a baby is born, they have around 300 bones in their body. Adults only have 206.

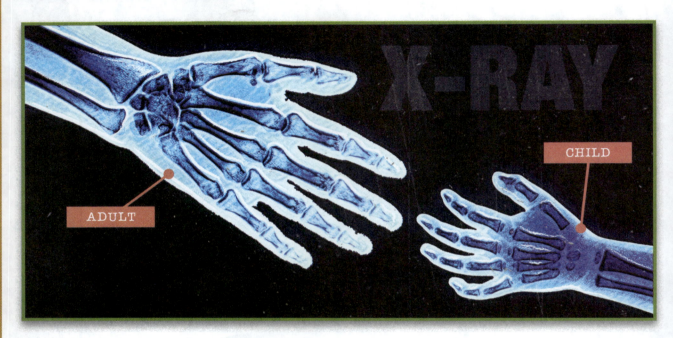

Why do babies have more bones than adults? Well, babies need to be much more flexible. In the womb when they're still growing, they must be all curled up. With more smaller bones, they can do just that.

FUN FACT

Where do you think the most bones in your body are located? Your hands! Each hand has 27 bones. (Your feet have 26 bones each.)

One bone that is absent from infants is the kneecap, or patella. It is made from cartilage and will become bone overtime. Babies' bones will fuse together. This means that two bones will join to become one. This process isn't fully complete until a person is 20 to 25 years old. Who knows how many bones you have right now!

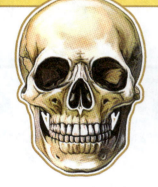

Use each word from the text in a sentence.

1. flexible

_____

2. process

_____

Answer the question.

3. What part of the body has the most bones?

 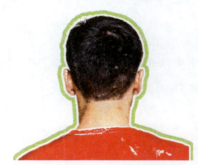 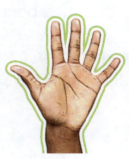

Write a response to the question.

4. Why does the author say adults don't have as many bones as babies?

_____

_____

_____

Solve each problem.

1. How many more bones do babies have than adults?

   _____ bones

2. For a person with two hands, how many total bones do they have in their hands?

   _____ bones

> GO BACK TO PAGE 112 IF YOU WANT TO KNOW WHY I'M SMILING.

3. If every person in a family of 4 people has two hands, how many total bones does this family have in their hands?

   _____ bones

4. On Saturday, New Life Hospital has 6 newborn babies sleeping in its nursery. How many total bones do those babies have?

   _____ bones

5. Some babies go home on Monday. The babies that are in the nursery now have a total of 1,200 bones. How many babies went home on Monday?

   _____ babies

Follow the directions.

Find and circle the piece that completes each bone. Write the number on the line. Then, write the numbers in order to answer the question.

Question: How many total bones are there in the hands and feet of an adult human?

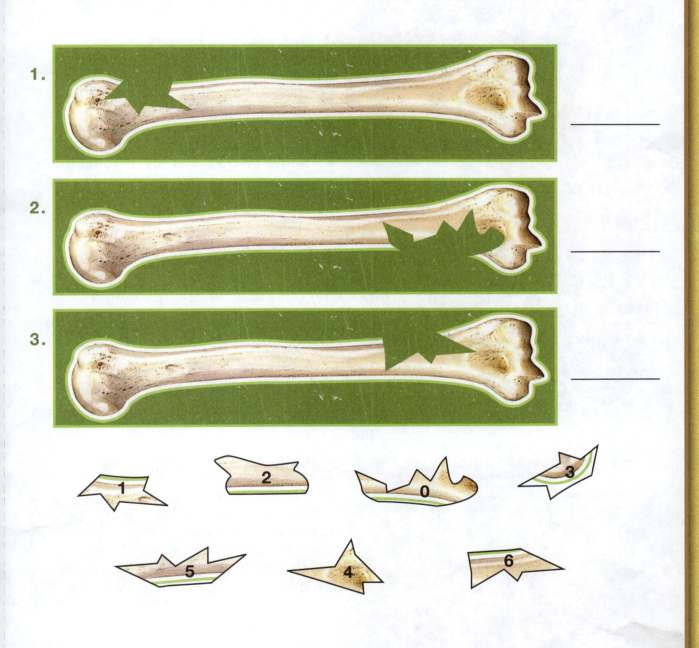

Answer: _____ _____ _____ bones

BUBBLE GUM BROCCOLI

Eating five servings of fruits and vegetables has been the advice of experts for years. But what if you don't like the taste of vegetables? A popular fast-food restaurant has got you covered.

In a wacky attempt to make broccoli more appealing, a popular fast food restaurant asked their food scientists to make the despised vegetable taste like something kids enjoy. Bubble gum-flavored broccoli was born. Does it sound like it tastes good to you? Well, it didn't. Kid taste-testers were confused by the taste. Flavored broccoli failed.

They weren't the only company to attempt this food trickery. One frozen french fries company created a line of fries that took on different shapes and colors. How about some blue fries? Or circular cocoa- and cinnamon-flavored fries? And you must have newly designed green ketchup to dip those fries in.

BLOWING BUBBLES WITH BROCCOLI IS HIGHLY DISCOURAGED

FUN FACT

McDonald's is the largest toy distributor in the world due to including toys in their Happy Meals. And, they've distributed more books than are housed at the Library of Congress.

Match each word to its definition.

1. popular   an added taste

2. despised   someone who knows a lot about a subject

3. expert   liked by many people

4. flavored   disliked something strongly

Write a response to each question.

5. What is this passage mostly about?

_____

_____

_____

6. Name two of the food products the companies created.

_____

_____

Solve each problem.

1. Fred's Fast Food made 45 orders of bubble gum broccoli. They sold only 15 orders of broccoli. How many orders of broccoli did they not sell?

   _____ orders of broccoli

2. Betty's Burgers sold only 18 orders of cocoa fries. They did not sell 32 orders of cocoa fries. How many orders of cocoa fries did they make in all?

   _____ orders of cocoa fries

3. Max's Made-to-Order Meals made 28 orders of blue fries. They had 21 orders not sold at the end of the day. How many orders of blue fries did they sell?

   _____ orders of blue fries

Follow the directions.

A popular fast-food restaurant asks you to come up with a new vegetable item for their menu. The vegetable must have a new color and a new flavor. Draw the picture of the new menu item and write a slogan for the new item describing its features.

Vegetable: _____

New Color: _____

New Flavor: _____

Slogan: _____

BET YOU CAN!

Would you, could you, write a book using only 50 words? If anyone could, it would be one of the most famous children's authors—Dr. Seuss.

Theodor Seuss Geisel wrote his popular children's book *The Cat in the Hat* using a list of 348 words created by educators to teach children to read. Dr. Seuss used only 236 of those words. His publisher at Random House, Bennett Cerf, made a bet with Seuss. Cerf bet Seuss $50 that he couldn't write a book with 50 or fewer distinct words.

The challenge ended with Dr. Seuss declared a winner. Cerf never paid up, but *Green Eggs and Ham* went on to be a best-selling and favorite book of children everywhere. Seuss admitted that he agonized over writing the book. He made vocabulary flow charts and used math to help him stick to 50 words.

In the end, Dr. Seuss was happy the book was selling, but even more important was that young readers loved it and were reading it.

 The German name Seuss is pronounced "Zoyce," but Dr. Seuss didn't mind that Americans pronounced it "Soose" because it rhymed with Mother Goose.

Answer each question.

1. In the passage, the word *bet* is used as a noun and a verb. Underline in red where *bet* is used as a verb. Underline in blue where *bet* is used as a noun.

2. What bet did Bennett Cerf and Dr. Seuss have?

   A. Cerf bet that Seuss couldn't write a book with only 236 words.

   B. Cerf bet that Seuss couldn't write a book with only 50 words.

   C. Cerf bet that Seuss couldn't write 50 more books.

Write a response to each question.

3. How did Dr. Seuss feel about writing *Green Eggs and Ham*? Use evidence from the text to support your answer.

   _____

   _____

   _____

4. Which book do you think was easier for Dr. Seuss to write? *Green Eggs and Ham* or *The Cat in the Hat*? Explain.

   _____

   _____

   _____

Use the graph to answer each question.

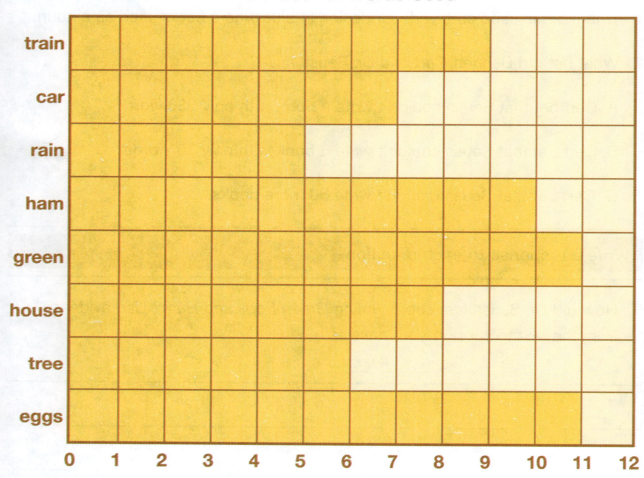

1. Of which two words did Dr. Seuss use the same amount?

   _____ and _____

2. How many times did he use the word *house*? _____

3. If he used the word *eat* 3 times more than *house*, then how many times did he use it in the book? _____

4. If he used the word *Sam* 18 times, which word did he use three times less in the book? _____

Follow the directions.

Use Dr. Seuss's 50-word list to write your own sentences. Cross off each word as you use it.

a	dark	house	on	them
am	do	I	or	there
and	eat	if	rain	they
anywhere	eggs	in	Sam	train
are	fox	let	say	tree
be	goat	like	see	try
boat	good	may	so	will
box	green	me	thank	with
car	ham	mouse	that	would
could	here	not	the	you

_____

_____

_____

_____

_____

_____

TOTALLY TOQUE

The French are known for gastronomy, the science of good eating. But they are also famous for their fashion. Put those together and you have a well-designed chef's uniform that is professional and functional. The chef's hat, or toque, is said to have 100 pleats. Why such a specific number?

The many folds are said to represent the number of ways the chef knew how to cook an egg. Or, it represented the number of recipes the chef knew how to cook. And the taller the toque, the higher the ranking in the kitchen. The toque, short for *toque blanche* (white hat), was made white to represent cleanliness. Its function remains clear—to keep hair out of a chef's eyes and out of the food they're preparing.

FUN FACT

Napoleon's army (also French) wore uniforms that were professional yet functional. Brass buttons were added to the sleeves to discourage soldiers from wiping tears, sweat, and boogers on them.

BANDANA

Most chefs still wear toques, especially when they are cooking in public. However, it is acceptable for modern kitchen staff to wear more common headgear such as baseball caps, headwraps, and bandanas.

Complete each sentence with a word from the word bank.

fashion	uniform	pleat

1. Each _____ is said to represent one way to cook an egg.

2. The French are famous for their _____ and good food.

3. A chef's _____ consists of a white toque, apron, and coat.

Answer each question.

4. What is the purpose of wearing a toque in a French kitchen?

   A. to be fashionable

   B. to keep hair out of a chef's eyes

   C. to brag about a chef's ranking among the kitchen staff

5. Which headgear does the author say modern chefs often wear?

   baseball cap   bow

   swim cap   headwrap

   top hat   cowboy hat

   bandana   helmet

Draw a line of symmetry through each symmetrical object.

From a bird's-eye view, a chef's toque has symmetry, which means it is the same on either side of a symmetrical line.

Follow the directions.

Each item of headgear is worth a different value from 1 to 5. Use the table to help you find the value of each.

 = _____   = _____

UNUSUALLY FUN READING & MATH GRADE 3

PERFECT PIZZA

Ask any kid what his or her favorite food is and you will most likely hear "Pizza!" screamed at several decibels above an inside talking voice. That child is probably imagining a large pizza with melty cheese and crispy pepperoni slices. But what about pineapple or barbeque chicken? Or fish and bananas? Some pizza toppings are just too bizarre to talk about. Especially if you just ate lunch. Did it happen to be pizza day in the school cafeteria?

In Costa Rica, coconut pizza is all the rage. Coconut adds a different texture to pizza that most Costa Ricans crave. In Russia, you'll find fish and onion pizza and in Sweden a curried banana pizza sprinkled with peanuts is on the menu. In Japan, squid and eel are the most popular pizza toppings.

No matter how you like your pizza, there are toppings for every craving. Just travel the globe and you will see (and smell) toppings that may turn your stomach or create a new favorite.

PEPPERONI PIZZA PERFECTION!

FUN FACT

In 1994, the first documented online purchase was made. Can you guess what was purchased? You got it—a pizza!

Write a sentence for each word. Use the part of speech given.

1. crave (*v*): _____

2. craving (*n*): _____

3. texture (*a*): _____

Write a response to each question.

4. Do you think the author likes pineapple or barbeque chicken on their pizza? Why or why not? Use evidence from the text to support your answer.

_____

_____

_____

5. Why do you think pizza toppings are different depending on where you live?

_____

_____

_____

6. Draw a picture of your favorite pizza and label the toppings.

Solve each problem.

1. Your school ordered 72 pizzas. Of the 72 pizzas, 24 are pepperoni. The other pizzas are cheese. How many cheese pizzas were ordered?

_____ cheese pizzas

2. What fraction of the pizzas ordered are pepperoni?

_____ of the pizzas are pepperoni

3. Papi's Pizza Palace makes 10 coconut pizzas, 7 banana pizzas, and 5 clam pizzas. If Papi's Pizza Palace cuts each pizza into 8 slices, how many slices of each pizza will they have?

_____ coconut pizza slices

_____ banana pizza slices

_____ clam pizza slices

Follow the directions.

What you need: paperclip, pencil

1. Put the paperclip on a toppings spinner, as shown.

2. Put the pencil inside the clip at the center point of the circle.

3. Hold the pencil. Flick the paperclip to spin.

4. Draw the topping on the pizza.

5. Repeat with each spinner.

What kind of pizza did you make? _____

UNUSUALLY FUN READING & MATH GRADE 3   147

ACCIDENTAL INVENTION

Pop! Pop! P-p-pop! Bubble Wrap's tiny bubbles of air are irresistible to human fingers. But, did you know that Bubble Wrap as we know it today was originally invented as wallpaper?

Inventors Alfred W. Fielding and Marc Chavannes made the textured wallpaper to appeal to a new generation of homeowners of the late 1950s. The inventors put two pieces of plastic shower curtain through a heat-sealing machine. The disappointing result was a sheet with trapped air bubbles.

Still, Fielding and Chavannes filed for patents for their invention and Sealed Air Corp. was born. They continued to devise more ways to use their invention—400 came to mind! Around the same time, IBM had come out with a computer that they wanted to safely ship. Bubble wrap was the answer to their problem.

More companies caught on and new forms of Bubble Wrap were being made that had different size bubbles, sheet lengths, and roll lengths.

One thing has stayed the same: the joy of popping the air-filled pockets is fun and stress-relieving!

 **FUN FACT** — Bubble Wrap has gone virtual! You can download an official Bubble Wrap app and pop virtual bubbles on the screen. Just as fun as popping the real thing? Maybe.

Match each word to its definition.

1. irresistible   to think of a way to do or create something

2. result   unable to resist

3. devise   something that is caused by something else

Write a response to each question.

4. How does the photo help you better understand the text?

_____

_____

5. What is another way to use Bubble Wrap? Explain.

_____

_____

Solve each problem.

1. IBM needs 6 feet of Bubble Wrap for each computer it ships. If IBM ships out 100 computers each day, how many feet of Bubble Wrap do they need?

   _____ feet

2. Cal's Calculators orders 246 feet of Bubble Wrap to ship their calculators. They need to return half of it. How much Bubble Wrap do they end up using?

   _____ feet

3. Dez's Doors wants Sealed Air Corp. to design a new sheet of Bubble Wrap for their doors. The wrap is 8 feet long and 4 feet wide. Each square foot needs to have 10 large bubbles. How many bubbles will be on the entire sheet of Bubble Wrap?

   _____ bubbles

Follow the directions.

Find each 9s fact in the Bubble Wrap. Write the products. The first one is done for you.

9 × 1 = __9__   9 × 6 = _____

9 × 2 = _____   9 × 7 = _____

9 × 3 = _____   9 × 8 = _____

9 × 4 = _____   9 × 9 = _____

9 × 5 = _____   9 × 10 = _____

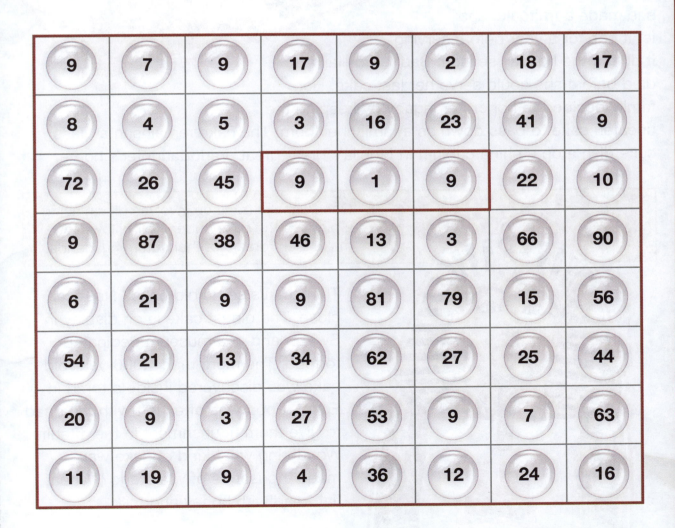

GRANDMA'S FRUITCAKE

We've all done it. We open the fridge scrounging for some leftovers. But how old is that foil-wrapped food? Most of us would look for mold or give it the sniff test. One family's fruitcake takes the cake for the most extreme leftover.

INDESTRUCTIBLE

The baker of the fruitcake, Fidelia Ford, made the cake in 1878. Every year she made a fruitcake and let it age for a year before serving it during the holiday season. Sadly, Fidelia died before she could serve her last cake. Her family decided to honor her legacy by keeping the uneaten cake to pass down as a family heirloom. The cake remains in a glass cake dish atop a china cabinet in Fidelia's great-great granddaughter's home.

FUN FACT

One fruitcake tradition involves girls placing a piece of the cake under their pillows to make them dream of their future husbands.

Think that's some old cake? Not even close. The oldest cake is on display in Switzerland in a museum dedicated to food. The more than 4,000-year-old cake was discovered inside a tomb in Egypt. Food was often left with the dead to give them nourishment in the afterlife. Wondering what kind of cake was made thousands of years ago? Wheat flatbread with honey and milk.

Match the word parts to make compound words from the text.

1. fruit   bread

2. flat   over

3. left   cake

Answer each question.

4. What does the author say is the reason Fidelia's family saved her fruitcake?

    A. They forgot about the cake.

    B. They wanted to honor her legacy.

    C. They wanted to eat it the next year.

5. Where was the oldest cake found?

    A. On top of a china cabinet

    B. In a museum

    C. In a tomb in Egypt

Write a response to the question.

6. Why do you think Fidelia's fruitcake has not gone bad?

_____

_____

Use the ingredient list for the fruitcake recipe to solve each problem.

Grandma's Fruitcake

2 cups water

2 cups sugar

2 cups raisins

$\frac{1}{2}$ cup butter

$\frac{1}{4}$ lb. candied orange peel

$\frac{1}{4}$ lb. candied citron

$\frac{1}{4}$ lb. candied red cherries

1 tbsp. crystallized ginger

$3\frac{1}{2}$ cups flour

1 tsp. baking soda

1 tsp. ground nutmeg

$\frac{1}{2}$ tsp. ground cloves

2 large eggs, beaten

1 tsp. vanilla extract

1. How many pounds (lb.) of candied fruit do you need for the recipe?

_____ pounds

2. How many teaspoons (tsp.) of cloves do you need for three fruitcakes?

_____ teaspoons

3. If you wanted to double the recipe, how many cups of flour would you need?

_____ cups

4. Divide the recipe in half. How much butter would you need?

_____ cup

Follow the directions.

Move only three fruitcakes to turn this pyramid upside down.

FAIRY FLOSS

CAVITY MAKER

Sugary, wispy, pastel cotton candy was invented by none other than a dentist!

Spun sugar has been around for centuries. But in 1897, a dentist named Dr. William Morrison teamed up with a candy maker named John Wharton. Together, they invented a machine that heated sugar in a spinning bowl. The bowl had tiny holes in it. The hot sugar made its way through the holes and turned into thin strands. The inventors called their treat *Fairy Floss*.

Dr. Morrison and Mr. Wharton introduced their machine at the St. Louis World's Fair in 1904. Fairy Floss was a hit! A candy store owner purchased their electric machine to make and sell fairy floss in his store. In 1949, Gold Medal Products began mass-producing the machines in their factory and selling them to stores.

FUN FACT — Around the world, cotton candy has different names. In the Netherlands it is called *Sugar Spider* and in China it is called *Dragon's Beard*.

Now, the sweet, melt-in-your-mouth treat is available all over the world at carnivals, fairs, festivals, and stores.

A BAGFUL OF HAPPINESS

Write a response to each question.

1. Why do you think a dentist invented a machine that would make candy?

   _____

   _____

2. What words does the author use to describe cotton candy? Can you come up with two more?

   _____

   _____

3. How is Fairy Floss made?

   _____

   _____

   _____

4. If you could give cotton candy a new name, what would it be? Why?

   _____

   _____

Skip count to complete the pattern.

1. At the St. Louis World's Fair, a box of Fairy Floss sold for one quarter or 25 cents. Skip count by 25s.

_____ _____ _____ _____ _____ _____ _____

Complete the table.

2. If the inventors sold 10 boxes in one day, how much money did they make? How about 100 boxes? Complete the table to show how much money they made for each number of boxes.

Number of Boxes	Amount Earned
1	25¢ or $0.25
10	
100	
1,000	
10,000	

Use a ruler or measuring tape to find objects.

3. The longest strand of fairy floss was measured at 1,400 meters long. Find objects that are about 1 meter long (100 cm). Write the name of three objects below. Just imagine what 1,400 of those end-to-end would look like!

_____ _____ _____

158 UNUSUALLY FUN READING & MATH GRADE 3

Follow the directions.

Design an advertisement for Fairy Floss to display at the St. Louis World's Fair in 1904. Draw and color your ad below. Include the price and write a slogan.

YELLOW MEANS STOP

When you see red, what do you think of? Do apples, fire engines, and cardinals come to mind? What about stop signs? But did you know that stop signs weren't always red?

In the early 20th century, traffic signs were all different shapes and colors. Drivers were often confused. So, the American Association of State Highway Officials (AASHO) decided to come up with a sign that would be used on all roads. A yellow octagon with "STOP" in black letters became the standard.

The association's first choice was red because red grabs your attention. The human eye sees red from farther away than other colors. Red is a longer wavelength of light. Yellow is a bit shorter. But the red dye available at the time faded quickly.

By the 1950s, sign makers were using fade-resistant porcelain enamel paints. Finally, red paint could be used and the red sign with "STOP" in white letters became standard.

 In the US, red means stop and green means go. But, in Japan, traffic lights use blue instead of green.

Write the definition of each word as it is used in the text.

1. standard: _____

2. confused: _____

Answer the question.

3. Which detail does not explain why the AASHO decided to make consistent signs for all highways?

   A. Traffic signs were all different shapes and colors.

   B. The human eye sees red from farther away.

   C. Drivers were often confused.

Write a response to each question.

4. In the text, what does the phrase *grabs your attention* mean?

   _____

5. Why were stop signs yellow before they were red? Use evidence from the text to support your answer.

   _____

   _____

   _____

Write a response to each question.

1. How are the signs' shapes similar? How are they different?

_____
_____

_____
_____

2. How are the signs' shapes similar? How are they different?

_____
_____

_____
_____

Name each shape.

3.  _____

4.   _____

5.   _____

Read each set of clues to draw the signs.

1. This sign has fewer than 5 sides.

   This sign has more than 3 corners.

   This shape has only one pair of parallel sides.

2. This sign has fewer than 6 corners.

   This sign has no parallel lines.

   This sign has more than 2 corners.

3. This sign has 0 straight sides.

   This sign has less than 3 corners.

   This sign looks like a clock face.

4. This sign has 4 equal sides.

   This sign has corners that are right angles.

   This sign has more than 3 corners.

KETCHUP AS MEDICINE

For thousands of years, ketchup has taken on many forms. Chinese sailors used a sauce they called *ge-tchup* or *keo-cheup*. But it was far from what we know ketchup is today.

Original recipes called for fish organs and salt left in a jar to ferment. As others took these recipes back to their own countries the recipes changed. With ingredients such as beer, walnuts, or mushrooms, ketchup was as different as people are around the world. Tomatoes weren't added until much later.

Once tomatoes were added to the recipes, vitamins and antioxidants made ketchup healthy. In the 1830s claims stated that ketchup cures diarrhea, indigestion, jaundice, and can even mend bones. Ketchup was even made into pills. However, most sellers of these pills made wild claims that anything that ails you could be cured with ketchup.

It was in 1876 that Henry Heinz produced the first bottle of Heinz ketchup made from tomatoes, vinegar, brown sugar, salt, and spices. No matter which ketchup you choose to put on your burgers and hot dogs, the puzzling fact remains: where do you thump the bottle to get that ketchup to come out? Thank goodness for squeeze bottles.

FUN FACT Before clean factories were mandatory, 90% of ketchup bottles contained ingredients that could harm someone who ate it.

Complete each sentence with a word from the word bank.

ferment	mend	harm	claims

1. Some sellers of ketchup medicine made _____ that it would cure upset stomachs.

2. People were told that ketchup could _____ broken bones.

3. Bottles used to contain things that could _____ someone who ate the ketchup.

4. Original ketchup recipes had fish and salt that was left to

_____ for a long time.

Write a response to each question.

5. What is the author's purpose for writing this passage? Explain.

_____

_____

_____

6. Do you like ketchup? Why or why not?

_____

_____

Use the information from each problem to solve the next problem.

1. Heinz Tomato Ketchup packs 8 bottles in each box they sell to stores. If you buy 6 boxes, how many bottles of ketchup will you have?

   _____ bottles

2. Heinz Tomato Ketchup packs 6 boxes in each crate they sell to stores. If you buy 7 crates, how many boxes of ketchup will you have?

   _____ boxes

3. You buy 4 crates of ketchup from Heinz Tomato Ketchup Company. You return 1 crate. How many boxes do you have left?

   _____ boxes

4. You buy 2 crates of ketchup from Heinz Tomato Ketchup Company in June and 3 crates of ketchup in July. How many bottles of ketchup did you buy in all?

   _____ bottles

Follow the directions.

Find each odd ketchup ingredient across, down, or diagonally in the puzzle.

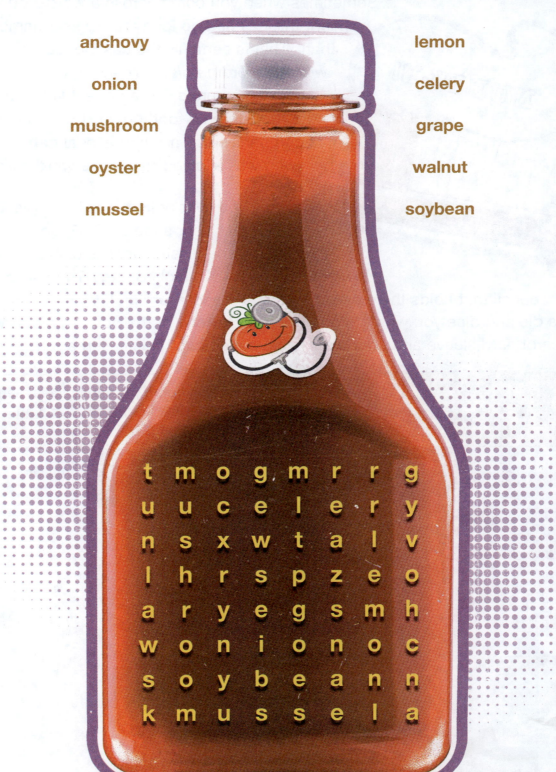

anchovy
onion
mushroom
oyster
mussel

lemon
celery
grape
walnut
soybean

t m o g m r r g
u u c e l e r y
n s x w t a l v
l h r s p z e o
a r y e g s m h
w o n i o n o c
s o y b e a n n
k m u s s e l a

WHATCHAMACALLIT?

Sometimes when you come across a word, you might think, "I had no idea there was a name for that!" That is certainly the case for some people with the word *nurdle*. Coined by advertisement agencies, a nurdle is the perfect little curve of toothpaste on a toothbrush. Two toothpaste companies actually had a legal battle over who was allowed to use the word *nurdle*.

Have you ever noticed the bit of plastic at the end of your shoelace? It's got a name too! That little plastic piece is called an *aglet*. How about another overlooked part? The part of a pencil that holds the eraser in place is called a *ferrule*. If you confuse the words die and dice you won't forget the name for one of the dots—a *pip*! And that cardboard sleeve around a disposable coffee cup? It is called a *zarf*.

> **FUN FACT**
> Here's a fun word! *Rhinotillexomania* means obsessive nose-picking. Now that's a mouthful, er, noseful!

RHINOTILLEXOMANIAC!

168

Match each word to its picture.

1. aglet

2. ferrule

3. zarf

4. pip

Write a response to each question.

5. Think of a new word for when gum gets stuck to your shoe. Use it in a sentence.

   _____

   _____

6. Think of a new word for the trail of goo left behind after someone wipes his nose on his sleeve. Use it in a sentence.

   _____

   _____

Write each number in expanded form.

1. There are 8,996 five-letter words in the dictionary.

   _____ + _____ + _____ + _____ = 8,996

2. There are 5,104 six-letter words in the dictionary.

   _____ + _____ + _____ = 5,104

3. There are 17,382 four-letter words in the dictionary.

   _____ + _____ + _____ + _____ + _____ = 17,382

Write each number word in standard form.

4. Six thousand, five hundred ninety-two

   _____

5. Fifty-four thousand, three hundred twenty-six

   _____

Follow the directions.

Read each clue. To figure out the word, cross out every other letter and write the remaining letters in order inside the boxes. Some of the letters are done for you.

1. the white crescent-shaped part of a fingernail

   A L B U C N D U E L F E

   | L | | N | | | |

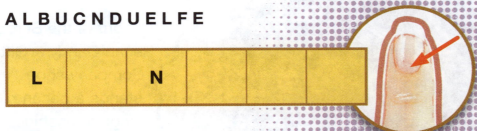

2. a group of ferrets

   G B H U I S J I K N L E M S N S

   | | U | | S | | | E | | | |

3. the swoosh sound silk ballgowns make

   O S P C Q R R O S O T P

   | | C | | | O | | |

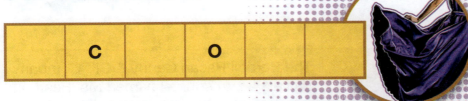

4. the indent on the bottom of a glass bottle

   V P W U X N Y T

   | | | N | |

PECAN PIE 24/7

Vending machines sure do come in handy. If you're hankering for a snack on a long road trip or are getting thirsty, vending machines can get you what you need fast! But snacks and drinks aren't the only things you can get out of a vending machine.

Out front of the Berdoll Pecan Candy & Gift Company shop stands a pecan pie vending machine! If you find yourself near Cedar Creek, Texas, make sure to stop by for a homemade pie from this 24-hour vending machine.

The shop's pies were in such high demand that they decided to create a way for customers to get their pies fast and at any time of day. The machine is restocked daily and even more often around the holidays.

FUN FACT

The Berdoll Pecan Candy & Gift Company has a 14-foot squirrel named Ms. Pearl on the property. But, don't worry. She's just a statue.

Write the definition of each word from the passage.

1. machine: _____

_____

2. demand: _____

_____

Answer the question.

3. Which is the best reason the Berdoll family installed a pecan pie vending machine outside their store?

A. They wanted to sell more pies and other goods.

B. They wanted to keep up with the high demand for their pies.

C. They wanted customers to come see Ms. Pearl.

Write a response to the question. Draw a picture.

4. If you could invent a vending machine for your room, what would it look like? What kinds of foods would it vend?

Solve each problem.

Berdoll Pecan Candy & Gift Co.	
Item	Price
Pecan Pie (with whole pecans)	$25.00
Pecan Pie (with chopped pecans)	$20.00
Chocolate Pecan Pie	$23.00
No-Added Sugar Pecan Pie	$22.00
1 Lb. Bag of Candied Pecans	$17.00
Assorted Pecan Tin	$30.00

1. You buy 3 chocolate pecan pies at the pecan shop. How much is your total?

$ _____

2. You spend $50 at the pecan shop. You buy two different items. What did you buy?

_____ and _____

3. You buy three items from the pecan shop. What is the least amount you could spend?

$ _____

Write your own problem using the information from the table. Solve it.

4. _____

_____

Follow the directions.

Read all the clues in order. Color the box red if the clue does not match. Color the box green if it does match. The first box has been done for you.

Peter, Paz, and Penny went to the pecan shop to eat dessert. The clerk mixed up their orders. Which dessert belongs to each person?

- Penny's dessert is melting.
- Peter is allergic to dairy.
- Paz does not like pretzels.

Explain your answer. _____

WACKY WARNINGS

Warning! Do not read this page while sleeping. Just kidding.

You've seen the words "Warning!" and "Caution!" on signs, buildings, and at construction sites. But what about on a toilet bowl brush? Bar of soap? No? Well, companies have had to add A LOT of warning labels on their products. They do this to avoid lawsuits. Some people incorrectly use products and then sue the company for money because they were injured. Here are some of the strangest warning labels.

Item	Warning
Toilet Bowl Brush	Do not use orally
Scooter	Warning—this object moves when used
Bar of Soap	Use like regular soap
Letter Opener	Safety goggles recommended
Snowblower	Do not use on roof
Birthday Candles	Do not use soft wax as earplugs
Collapsible Baby Stroller	Remove child before folding
Public Toilet	Water unsafe for drinking
Iron	Do not iron clothes while they are being worn
Wheelbarrow	Not intended for highway use
TV Remote Control	Not dishwasher safe

And that superhero costume you want for next Halloween? Be warned: "It will not enable flight or super strength." Bummer.

Fireplace logs carry this warning: "Caution—risk of fire." And that stick lighter? Well, its label reads "Do not use near fire, flame, or sparks." Huh?

Answer each question.

1. Companies added warning labels to

A. help consumers know how to use a product.

B. avoid lawsuits against them.

C. take up space on product packaging.

2. What is the meaning of the word *sue* as used in the text?

A. A woman's name

B. To caution

C. To seek justice

Write a response to each question.

3. What do you think a person did that resulted in adding the warning to all wheelbarrows?

_____

_____

4. Which warning label do you think is the most ridiculous? Explain.

_____

_____

Solve each problem.

1. Clumsy Cliff sued Acme Products for $2,000. He won half of the money. How much did he win?

   $ _____

2. Betsy Butterfingers sued Joe's Diner for $12,000. She won a third of the money. How much did she win?

   $ _____

3. Grace Less sued Handy Hal's Hardware for $8,000. She won three-fourths of the money. How much did she win?

   $ _____

Write a wacky warning for each product.

"HIGHEST COURT"

While Supreme Court justices are passing judgements on cases, employees a few floors above might be passing a basketball back and forth in a pick-up game of hoops. That's right, the Supreme Court of the United States has its own full basketball court!

Jokingly named the "Highest Court in the Land," the basketball court and gym on the fifth floor of the Supreme Court Building was built in the 1940s. Originally, the basketball court featured wooden backboards and a concrete floor. Since then, it has been updated with plexiglass backboards and a hardwood floor that has the majestic eagle of the Supreme Court on full display.

This court is not in session when the actual Supreme Court on the second floor is in session. The bouncing of the ball, people running up and down the court, and the dropping of weights can be heard in the courtroom below. As a sign outside the gym reads, *"The laws of the land take priority over games of pick-up basketball."*

The first baskets used for basketball were peach baskets. And the first ball? A soccer ball.

Complete each sentence with a homophone from the word bank.

| court | justice |

1. "_____ is now in session!" the judge declared.

2. Our school got a new basketball _____.

3. All people deserve _____.

4. The president nominated a new Supreme Court _____.

Write a response to each question.

5. What is the main idea of this passage?
   _____
   _____

6. Why do you think there is a rule that no one can play basketball while the Supreme Court is in session?
   _____
   _____

UNUSUALLY FUN READING & MATH GRADE 3

Solve each problem.

1. On Mondays, 4 teams of 5 people play basketball. How many people play basketball on Monday?

_____ people

2. On Tuesday, 30 people play basketball. If each team has 5 people, how many teams play on Tuesday?

_____ teams

Answer each question.

3. Ruth's basketball team plays 4 times in one week. Of the 4 games, they win 3. What is Ruth's team's win record as a fraction?

A. $\frac{1}{2}$

B. $\frac{3}{4}$

C. $\frac{4}{3}$

4. The next week, Ruth's basketball team plays 4 more times. Of those games, they win 1. What is Ruth's team's win record over the two weeks as a fraction?

A. $\frac{1}{2}$

B. $\frac{3}{8}$

C. $\frac{1}{8}$

Follow the directions.

There are nine US Supreme Court justices, one chief justice and eight associate justices. Find the names of the current Supreme Court justices in the word search.

JOHN G. ROBERTS JR.   **NEIL M. GORSUCH**

CLARENCE THOMAS   **BRETT M. KAVANAUGH**

SAMUEL A. ALITO   **AMY CONEY BARRETT**

SONIA SOTOMAYOR   **KETANJI BROWN JACKSON**

ELENA KAGAN

```
U Y N I R O N E I L M G O R S U C H S R
I N S P H H B E U R H N M P V U M K E U
Z C X O P J O H N G R O B E R T S J R S
K E T A N J I B R O W N J A C K S O N A
B R Z D S I F W C S H B N K Y O Q Q Q M
X R F C A F A P C D V Q P K Y P Y Q C U
Y R E S C V X S W O R Q P N Z Q F R J E
P R G T H L K I O L H W T A E J Z U P L
W U Q T T H A Y M T F R N A V R M Y G A
E P S A E M U R D D O W C M F W J E Z A
T Z J P L M K W E Z Z M C Z N F G V X L
Q H Q V E C H A M N A H A R D J J G D I
K H B Q N H G E V O C W T Y N T J M F T
Z M R W A M A E V A A E A P O J T L E O
S J E V K S W P W H N X T C N R S P A T
P J X H A P V K E M K A O H F T Q V S B
A Q O U G Z L J W C M T U H O G E Y B Z
L N Q D A P S J X Q R O B G J M U L T R
K E M I N I L B T F Y P I X H O A Q D G
G A M Y C O N E Y B A R R E T T W S L V
```

UNUSUALLY FUN READING & MATH GRADE 3

ROCKIN' ROADS

There are almost 50,000 miles of interstate highways that connect cities and states across the United States. They all serve the same purpose—to get people from one place to another. But there are highways in the United States that also serve another purpose—to make the road trip a little more musical.

Small, well-placed rumble strips are behind these musical highways. Normally used to warn motorists to slow down, these rumble strips create vibrations with a car's tires that echo a song.

One such road is located in Lancaster, California. This road treats motorists to a version of the *William Tell Overture* if they drive over it at exactly 50 miles per hour. Originally, this musical highway was located in a residential area. As it became popular and busy, neighbors complained of the traffic and noise. It is now located in a more rural area where only passing cars can hear it.

FUN FACT Highway signs are green because cool colors don't distract drivers like caution signs in red, orange, and yellow.

Complete each sentence with a word from the word bank.

overture	interstate	residential	motorist

1. An _____ highway is a highway connecting two or more states.

2. A person who travels using an automobile can be called a _____.

3. The opening part of a song played by an orchestra is an _____.

4. A _____ neighborhood is a neighborhood where people live.

Write a response to each question.

5. Would you want a musical highway near your home? Why or why not?

_____

_____

_____

6. Where was the musical highway originally located in Lancaster, California, and why was it moved?

_____

_____

_____

Solve each problem.

(Hint: Speed × Time = Distance)

1. Anya is driving 6 miles to work and going 30 miles per hour. How long would a song need to be to last Anya's entire trip?

   0.2 hours or _____ minutes

2. Kai has a playlist of 10 songs. Each song is 3 minutes long. If he is traveling at 60 miles per hour, for how many miles will his playlist last?

   _____ miles

Take a survey. Record the results.

3. You're in charge of choosing a song for a new musical highway! Choose three songs. Ask family and/or friends to vote for one of the songs. Make a bar graph to show their responses.

Which song won? _____

186

Follow the directions.

Drive through the maze to get to Route 66. Write the letters you cross in order on the lines below to finish the fun fact!

There was another musical highway in the US located on the famous Route 66! Driving 45 miles per hour over this stretch of highway played this song:

" __ __ __ __ __ __ __ __ __ __

__ __ __ __

__ __ __ __ __ __ __ __ __ "

PINK LAKES

When you think pink, what comes to mind? Bubblegum, flamingoes, or cotton candy, right? But what about a lake?

The most well-known pink lake in the world is Lake Hillier in Australia. It is surrounded by a lush green forest, and just beyond that is the beautiful blue waters of the Pacific Ocean. The contrast of nature's blue and green hues next to the incredible bright pink water of Lake Hillier make it the most photographed pink lake in the world.

You're probably wondering, if water appears blue, then how are these lakes pink? While each pink lake and each region where they are located is different, scientists have identified mostly salt, bacteria, microbes, and algae as the magicians behind this color-changing wonder.

LAKE HILLIER

FUN FACT Oceans aren't really blue. Water acts like a filter. It soaks up all the colors except for blue. The blue left behind is the only color for our eyes to see.

ALTERED STATE

The presence of these things alters the color of the water and creates a feast for our eyes. To date, scientists have found almost 50 pink lakes scattered around the world.

188

UNUSUALLY FUN READING & MATH GRADE 3

Match each word to its definition.

1. lush   in comparison to something else

2. contrast   a color

3. hue   a germ or microorganism

4. microbe   growing in a healthy way

Write a response to each question.

5. Do you think the author likes or dislikes pink lakes?

_____

6. List two reasons you came to this conclusion.

_____

_____

_____

Solve each problem.

1. On Friday, 7 tour busses with 8 people in each tour bus visit a pink lake. How many people visit the lake in all?

   _____ people

2. On Saturday, 4 tour busses with 10 people on each bus visit a pink lake. Twenty of those visitors get a picture with the lake. How many visitors do not get a picture with the lake? Write your answer as a fraction.

   _____ of the visitors

3. On Sunday, 27 people get on 3 tour busses to go to the lake. There are an equal number of people on each bus. One of the tour busses gets a flat tire and doesn't make it to the lake. How many people visit the lake on Sunday?

   _____ people

Use the information from above to create a bar graph.

4. Make a bar graph showing the number of visitors for Friday, Saturday, and Sunday.

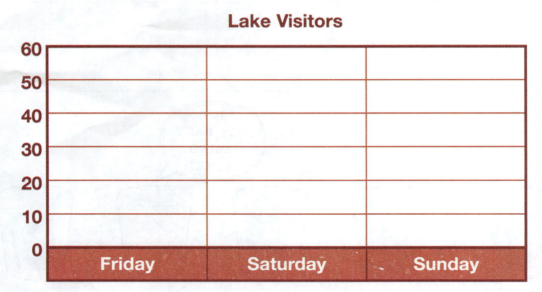

Find the names of some of the world's pink lakes in the word search.

LAKE HILLIER

LAKE RETBA

HUTT LAGOON

DUSTY ROSE LAKE

LAKE NATRON

LAKE MASAZIR

LAS COLORADAS

```
D H H E J N N Y L A K E N A T R O N O P
S U F D O I F V M Y Y L H G B G F K L L
B T S J K Y P K J L Q E R T Y U I O M A
X T K T N U O P H A W D F G H J J L N K
Y L D R Y F I O G K G H J A Z X C V B E
H A J S F R U I F E Q W C V B N M K O R
J G S D L G O M M H D E R D G H I O I E
O O J K P H U S N I T Y U J K M D Z J T
L O N P Q C Y U E L A V N R T Y A O P B
A N F I W V T Y C L R T N M K S I U O A
G Y K S G B W T V I A G K A A K D F V B
T R N K J N E R B E R K U M L K Q W E R
L U F F B M S E N R M J E E R T Y U I O
K H S L H Y D W M C N K L K J O I S D F
P T F I J U F Q Z X A G H J K L K T Y O
Q G M Y L A S C O L O R A D A S D G L P
```

UNUSUALLY FUN READING & MATH GRADE 3

TREE HOUSE VILLAGES

Do you have a tree house in your backyard? Or maybe you have seen a tree house on TV? Tree houses are fun! Sitting amongst the trees, you get to see everything from a different perspective. Now imagine packing your bags and setting off on a trip where your destination is a tree house that you are going to stay in!

There are many places around the United States where you can book a vacation in a tree house. Tree house villages are perfect for people who want to get away for a quiet, relaxing vacation in nature without all the work of camping.

FUN FACT

If you want to camp but don't want to rough it, try glamping! It's camping but with all the amenities you need to keep you comfy. Glamour + Camping = Glamping.

Tree house villages have tree houses of all shapes and sizes. Some are small and simple. They might include a bed, a living area with furniture, and a small sink. Other tree houses have multiple bedrooms, a larger living area, a kitchen, and even a bathroom—everything you need for a complete vacation. While most people who visit a tree house village are wanting to unplug from their busy life and enjoy the peace and quiet of nature for a while, some tree houses have TVs and Wi-Fi. This could come in handy if it's raining.

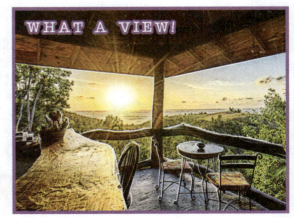

WHAT A VIEW!

192   UNUSUALLY FUN READING & MATH GRADE 3

Write a response to each question.

1. Who does the author suggest might want to stay in a tree house village for vacation?

_____

_____

2. What are two things a tree house might include?

_____

_____

3. Draw your ideal tree house. Label at least four features.

UNUSUALLY FUN READING & MATH GRADE 3

Solve each problem.

1. Mateo is staying with his family in a tree house for vacation. The length of the tree house is 12 feet, and the width is 8 feet. What is the area of the tree house?

   _____ square feet

2. Naomi is staying in the same tree house village. The tree house her family is staying in has two different sections. The length of the first section is 11 feet, and the width is 9 feet. The length of the second section is 10 feet, and the width is 10 feet. What is the total area of Naomi's tree house?

   _____ square feet

3. What is the difference in square feet between Mateo and Naomi's tree houses?

   _____ square feet

4. Below is the floor plan for one of the tree houses. What is the area?

   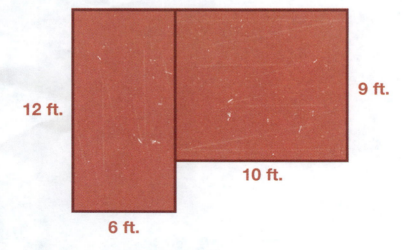

   _____ square feet

Find your way to the tree house village. Follow the path counting by 7s.

ICEHOTEL

One of the coolest places you could ever spend the night is at the Icehotel in Sweden. Carved out of ice and snow, visitors will feel like they are guests in a magnificent ice palace.

Anyone who is staying at the Icehotel in the winter must like cold weather. The rooms in the hotel are a chilly 18-23 degrees Fahrenheit. Every visitor is given warm boots, a snowsuit, and a sleeping bag to sleep in. To help take the chill off the bed made of ice, it is topped with a mattress and then reindeer hides for warmth.

Because people are not polar bears, the Icehotel does offer a chance to thaw out when needed. There is a warm lobby next to the hotel where guests can relax in a sauna, take a hot shower, get dressed, and have breakfast in the morning. Guests can also wander around the art and design gallery that features magnificent ice sculptures made by local artists.

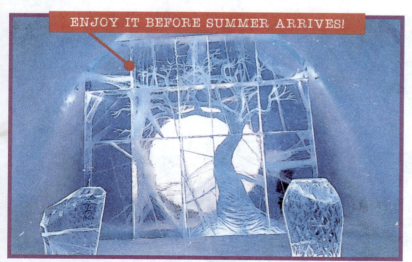

ENJOY IT BEFORE SUMMER ARRIVES!

FUN FACT — This hotel is carved fresh every winter and melts away every spring.

Answer each question.

1. What is the temperature of the rooms in the Icehotel?

    A. 25–30 degrees Fahrenheit

    B. 18–23 degrees Celsius

    C. 18–23 degrees Fahrenheit

2. What does the Icehotel offer guests who want to warm up?

    A. Warm showers

    B. A gallery with ice sculptures

    C. A sauna

    D. Both A and C

Write a response to each question.

3. Why does the author say, "Anyone who is staying at the Icehotel in the winter has to like cold weather"?

    _____

    _____

4. Do you think the Icehotel gives visitors enough supplies to keep warm in one of their rooms? Why or why not?

    _____

    _____

    _____

Solve each problem.

1. Leilani is staying at the Icehotel. Her room is 4 times colder than the lobby. The lobby is 72 degrees Fahrenheit. What is the temperature of Leilani's room?

   _____ degrees Fahrenheit

2. Ian is handing out blankets to guests at the Icehotel. He hands out 48 blankets to 12 guests. If each guest took the same number of blankets, how many blankets does each guest have?

   _____ blankets

3. There are ice rooms and warm rooms at the Icehotel. In one weekend there are 100 guests at the Icehotel. Of the guests, 16 stayed in a warm room. The rest of the guests stayed in an ice room. Half of the guests who stayed in an ice room visited the sauna. How many guests stayed in an ice room but did not visit the sauna?

   _____ guests

Use the code to reveal the fun fact.

1	2	3	4	5	6	7	8	9	10	11	12	13
A	B	C	D	E	F	G	H	I	J	K	L	M

14	15	16	17	18	19	20	21	22	23	24	25	26
N	O	P	Q	R	S	T	U	V	W	X	Y	Z

What might you see if you stay at the Icehotel in the fall?

__ __ __
20 8 5

__ __ __ __ __ __ __
14 15 18 20 8 5 18 14

__ __ __ __ __
12 9 7 8 20 19

NATURE'S NIGHT-LIGHT

UNUSUALLY FUN READING & MATH GRADE 3

A TOWN WITH NO NAME

Every city and town in the United States is unique. But when it comes to names, some cities are more unique than others!

Don't feel bad for this Colorado town. It does have a name, it just sounds like it doesn't. When a city worker temporarily labeled a new exit off a highway as "No Name," he didn't mean for it to stick. But as the sign remained there and residents got used to it, they ended up liking it and making the name official.

CAUTION! HOT!

Hot Coffee, Mississippi, used to be the half-way point between two popular travel destinations in the South. To lure travelers to his store, a man named L.N. Davis hung a coffee pot outside and advertised "the best hot coffee around." It worked! Travelers loved his coffee, and the locals named the town after him.

What happens when people argue back and forth and can't come to an agreement on something? A town is named Whynot. This is what happened in a North Carolina town in the 1800s. In a town meeting, locals couldn't agree on a name for the town, so someone said, "Why not name the town Whynot?" They all agreed and went home.

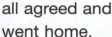

DESTINATION MEH

FUN FACT — A trip to Boring, Maryland, sure doesn't sound exciting. It just happens that this town was named after its first postmaster, David Boring.

Match each word to its definition.

1. lure   during a limited time

2. temporarily   something unlike anything else

3. official   something authorized

4. unique   to attract something strongly

Write a response to each question.

5. How did Hot Coffee, Mississippi, get its name?

_____

_____

_____

6. How did Whynot, North Carolina, get its name?

_____

_____

_____

Solve each problem.

1. Wes is making a new welcome sign for the town hall door in No Name, Colorado. Help him figure out the perimeter of the new sign.

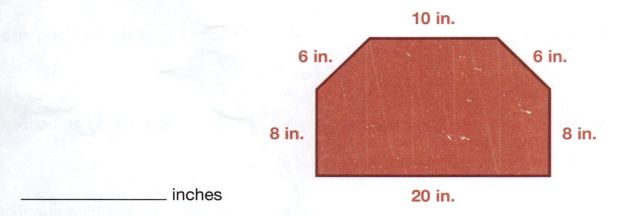

_____ inches

2. A trip from Whynot, North Carolina, to Boring, Maryland, is 408 miles. A trip from Whynot, North Carolina, to Hot Coffee, Mississippi, is 705 miles. What is the difference in miles between the two trips?

5 MINUTES INTO THE TRIP AND YOU ALREADY HAVE TO GO TO THE BATHROOM?

_____ miles

3. You are driving from Whynot, North Carolina, to Boring, Maryland. After 2 hours, you stop for a break. You have driven 96 miles. How fast have you been driving in miles per hour? (Hint: Distance ÷ Time = Speed)

_____ miles per hour

Follow the directions.

You are designing five new signs for your town. The signs must be rectangles. Each sign must have an area greater than 15 square feet and less than 30 square feet. Draw your signs below.

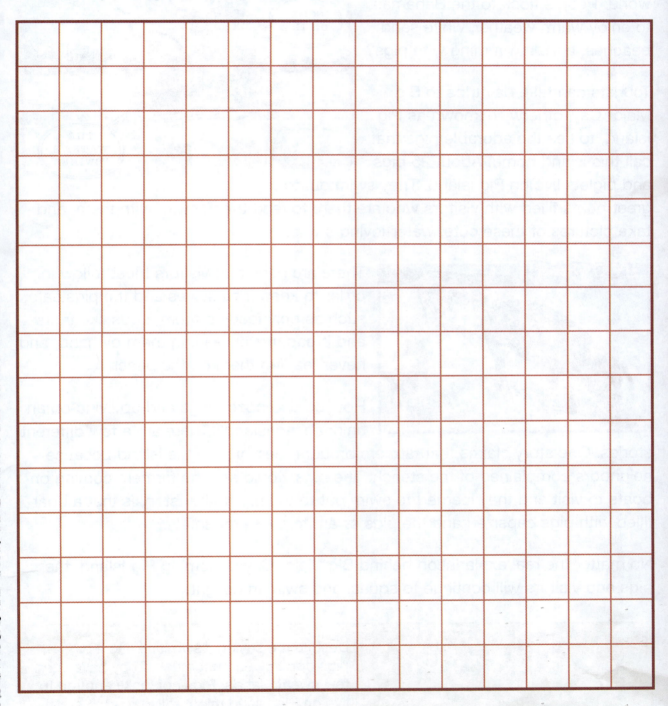

1 square unit = 1 square foot

PIG ISLAND

The Bahamas are known as some of the most beautiful islands in the world. People flock to the Bahamas to enjoy warm weather, white sand beaches, and…swimming with pigs?

Tourists can take day trips to Big Major Cay, otherwise known as Pig Island, to see the adorable pigs that call this island home. About 25 pigs and piglets live on Pig Island. They swim out to greet boats filled with visitors who are there to feed them, swim with them, and take pictures of these cute, water-loving swine.

There are rules that visitors must follow in order to keep themselves and the pigs safe, such as only feeding them foods like fruits and bread, never feeding them by hand, and never feeding them on the beach.

How do two dozen pigs end up living on an uninhabited island? There are a few different stories. One story claims that farmers brought their pigs to the island because neighbors complained of the stench. The pigs would see the farmers coming on boats to visit and they learned to swim out to them. Another story is that a boat filled with pigs capsized and the pigs swam to shore for safety.

No matter the real explanation behind Big Major Cay becoming Pig Island, the pigs and visitors will continue to squeal and swim in delight.

FUN FACT

Despite the saying, "sweating like a pig," pigs don't sweat that much. They have very few sweat glands. Pigs not lucky enough to live on Pig Island might roll in mud to stay cool.

Match each word to its definition.

1. flock   a pig

2. swine   a place that is not lived in by people

3. uninhabited   to overturn

4. capsized   to come together in a large group

Write a response to each question.

5. Name two of the rules visitors must follow to keep themselves and the pigs safe.

_____

_____

_____

6. What is one of the explanations for how the pigs came to live at Pig Island?

_____

_____

_____

_____

Solve each problem.

1. There are 25 pigs on Pig Island. Fourteen of the pigs are female. Of the 14, half are piglets. How many female piglets are on Pig Island?

   _____ female piglets

2. How many of the pigs on Pig Island are male?

   _____ male pigs

3. A farmer wants to bring his pigs to Pig Island so they can learn to swim. He has 13 female pigs and 16 male pigs. If he brings his pigs to Pig Island, how many female and male pigs would there be? How many total pigs would there be?

   _____ female pigs

   _____ male pigs

   _____ total pigs

Follow the directions.

Read the clues to find the answers. Write the name of each pig under their picture.

- Otis is the biggest pig on the beach, but he's not the tallest.

- Blossom might not be the biggest, but she is the tallest.

- Sebastian isn't just one color.

- Pearl is the smallest pig of them all.

_____ _____

_____ _____

ICE CREAM GRAVEYARD

Have you heard the saying, "All good things must come to an end"? This is true even for ice cream flavors. Like most foods, there are popular flavors of ice cream, and not-so-popular flavors of ice cream. Flavors like vanilla, cookie dough, and birthday cake are common favorites. But for the unpopular, Ben & Jerry's Ice Cream has created the Flavor Graveyard.

Could the name be the culprit in the death of some of the flavors in the Flavor Graveyard? That might have been the case for the unappetizing Turtle Soup and Wavy Gravy. Or maybe it was the actual taste? The ginger-flavored ice cream in Miz Jelena's Sweet Potato Pie might not have been for everyone. Or Sugar Plum made with plum ice cream.

Luckily for the ice cream flavors lying peacefully in the Flavor Graveyard, Ben & Jerry's believes in second chances. Customers can submit a *Resurrect This Flavor* form on their website telling them why they believe one of these flavors deserves to rise again. Maybe one of your Flavor Graveyard favorites will be given a second chance?

FUN FACT

Waffle cones, or *cornucopias* as they were called, made their debut at the 1904 St. Louis World's Fair.

CORNUCOPIA OF DELICIOUS GOODNESS

Answer the question.

1. What is the main idea of the passage?

A. Popular ice cream flavors sell out at Ben and Jerry's ice cream stores.

B. Unpopular ice cream flavors are sold at a discount by Ben and Jerry's ice cream stores.

C. Unpopular ice cream flavors are taken off shelves and "buried" in the Flavor Graveyard.

Write a response to each question.

2. Do you think the author likes the sound of the ice cream flavor Wavy Gravy? Why or why not?

_____

_____

3. Which ice cream from the passage that is in the Flavor Graveyard would you most want to try? Draw a new label for the flavor and give it a new name.

Solve each problem.

1. If 5 ice cream flavors are laid to rest each year, how many new flavors would be in the Flavor Graveyard in 4 years?

SO YUMMY!

_____ flavors

2. Olivia loved the flavor Peanut Butter and Jelly, but it's in the Flavor Graveyard now. She wants to save the flavor, so she sends a form to resurrect the flavor 3 times a week for 9 weeks. How many times does Olivia send a form in all?

SHERBETLICIOUS!

_____ times

3. If 32 flavors are in the Flavor Graveyard and there are 8 rows of headstones, how many flavors are in each row?

CHOCO GOODNESS!

_____ flavors

Follow the directions.

Solve the crossword puzzle. Then, write the answers on the lines to name more flavors in the Flavor Graveyard.

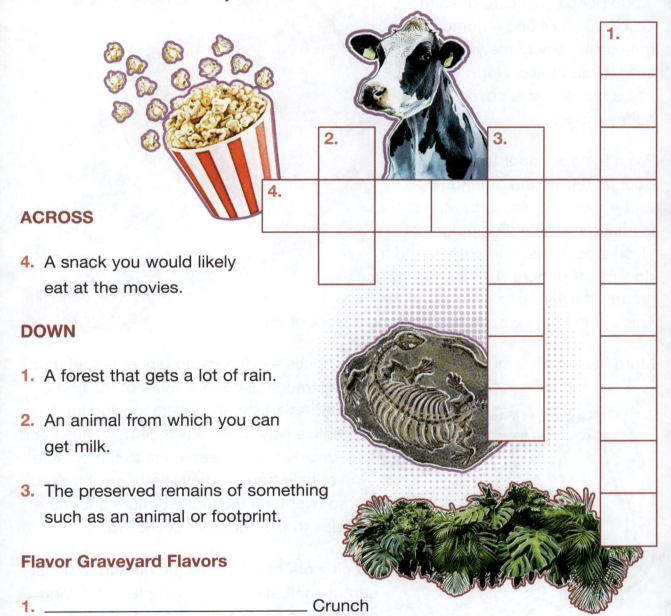

ACROSS

4. A snack you would likely eat at the movies.

DOWN

1. A forest that gets a lot of rain.

2. An animal from which you can get milk.

3. The preserved remains of something such as an animal or footprint.

Flavor Graveyard Flavors

1. _____ Crunch

2. _____ Power

3. _____ Fuel

4. Peanuts! _____ !

HOUSE OF MUGS

In a small town of a little more than 1,000 people in western North Carolina, you'll find a home that is truly unlike any home you've ever seen. Collettsville, North Carolina, has a home that is covered in coffee mugs.

From the front door to the back door, and from the ground up to the roof, the House of Mugs is adorned with coffee mugs of all shapes, sizes, and colors. And it doesn't stop there. The fence that goes around the yard is covered in mugs too. This cabin in the woods has become a work of art!

LOOK! A HOUSE IN A MUG!

More than 20,000 mugs are nailed to the house's exterior and fence. It started 20 years ago with just 15 mugs that the owners of the home had bought. As artists, they were looking for a creative way to display their new mugs and decided to nail each one to the outside of their house. They liked how it looked, so over time they added more and more mugs to their outdoor collection.

Their work of art slowly turned into a tourist attraction. It started with people just driving by, but some people also started sneaking their own mugs onto the home. Since then, the owners have encouraged it, if you can find an empty spot!

FUN FACT — Ancient mugs were made from carved wood or bone, or shaped clay.

Match each word to its definition.

1. adorned   gave support

2. exterior   decorated or made beautiful

3. attraction   the outside of something

4. encouraged   a place that draws visitors

Write a response to each question.

5. What is the main idea of this passage?

_____

_____

6. Write two facts that support the main idea.

_____

_____

_____

UNUSUALLY FUN READING & MATH GRADE 3

Solve each problem.

1. One year 952 mugs are added to the House of Mugs. The next year, 1,124 mugs were added. How many more mugs were added the second year than the first?

   _____ mugs

2. On one wall, there are 5 rows of mugs. If there are 9 mugs in each row, how many mugs are on the wall?

   _____ mugs

3. On another wall, there are 100 mugs. If there are 10 rows of mugs, how many mugs are in each row?

   _____ mugs

4. If 7 people visit the House of Mugs on one day and add a total of 28 new mugs, how many mugs did each person add if they each added an equal amount?

   _____ mugs

Each mug was printed backwards! Write the words on the lines.

1. _____

2. _____

3. _____

4. _____

Answer Key

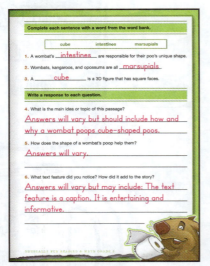

Page 5

Page 6

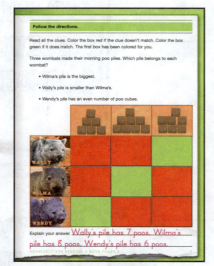

Page 7

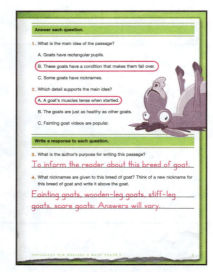

Page 9

Answer Key

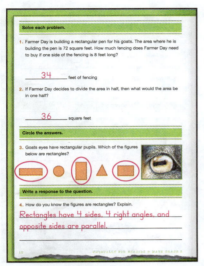
Page 10

Page 11

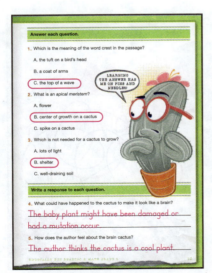
Page 13

Page 14

Answer Key

Page 15

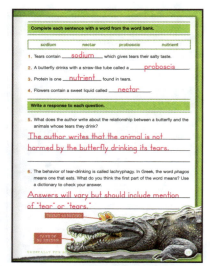

Page 17

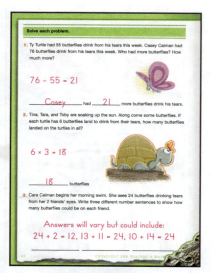

Page 18

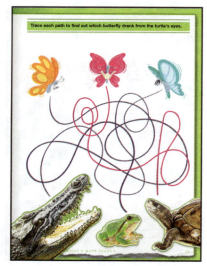

Page 19

Answer Key

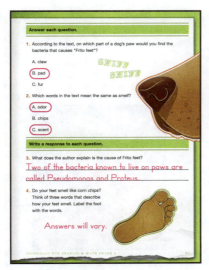

Page 21

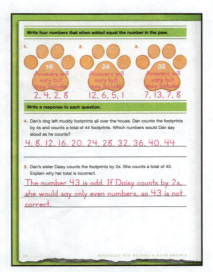

Page 22

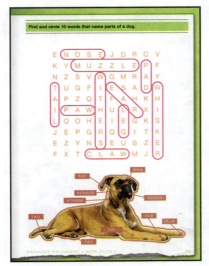

Page 23

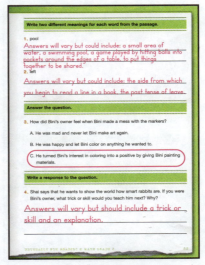

Page 25

Answer Key

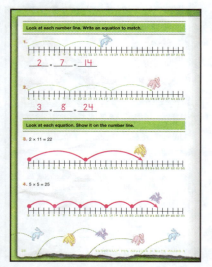
Page 26

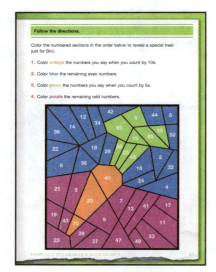
Page 27

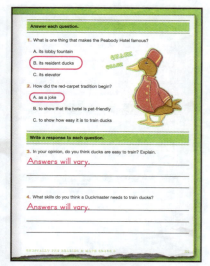
Page 29

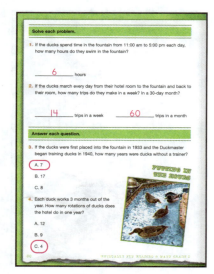
Page 30

Answer Key

Page 31

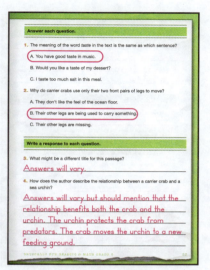

Page 33

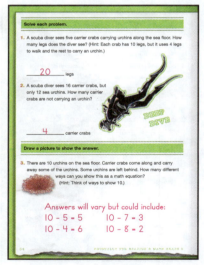

Page 34

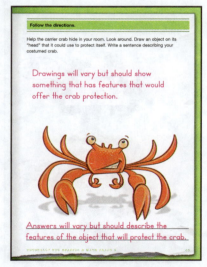

Page 35

Answer Key

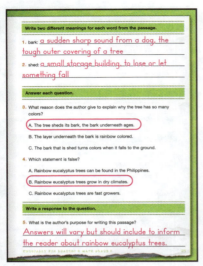
Page 37

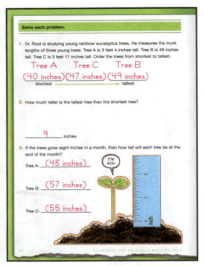
Page 38

Page 39

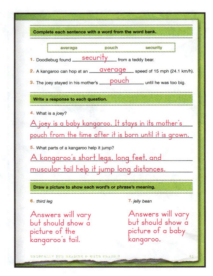
Page 41

Answer Key

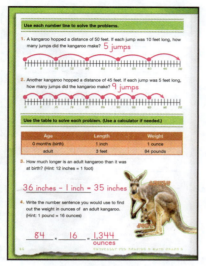

Page 42

Page 43

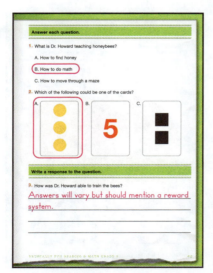

Page 45

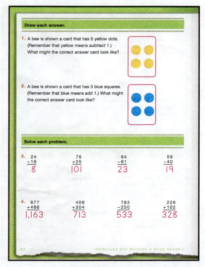

Page 46

Answer Key

Page 47

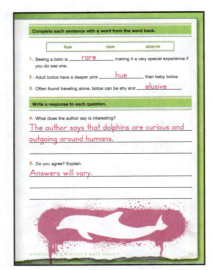

Page 49

Page 50

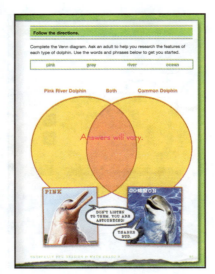

Page 51

Answer Key

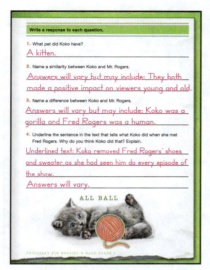
Page 53

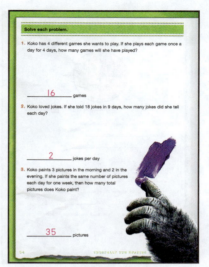
Page 54

Page 55

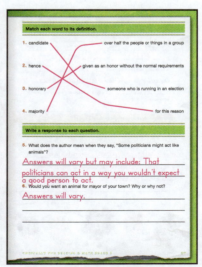
Page 57

Answer Key

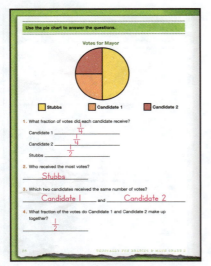

Page 58

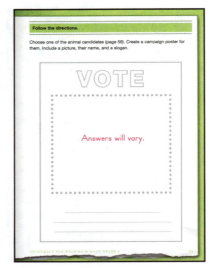

Page 59

Page 61

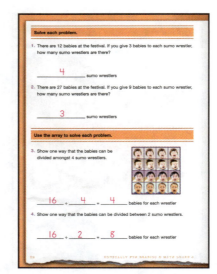

Page 62

Answer Key

Page 63

Page 65

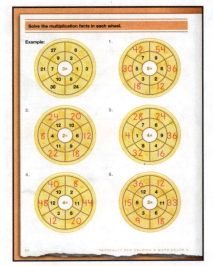

Page 66

Page 67

Answer Key

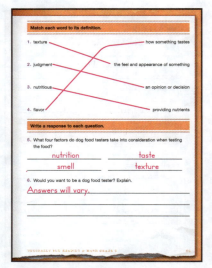
Page 69

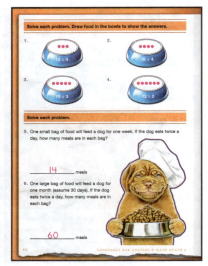
Page 70

Page 71

Page 73

Answer Key

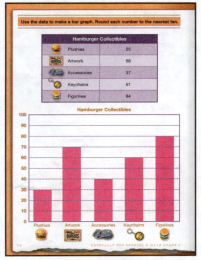

Page 74

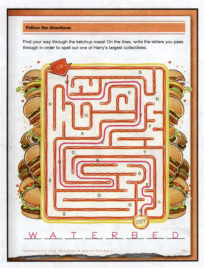

Page 75

Page 77

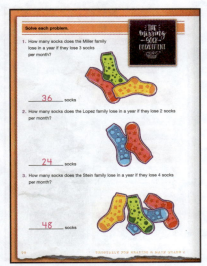

Page 78

Answer Key

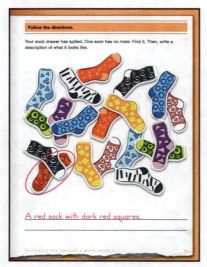
Page 79

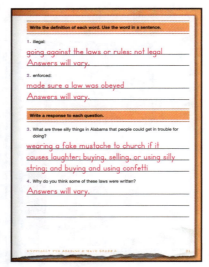
Page 81

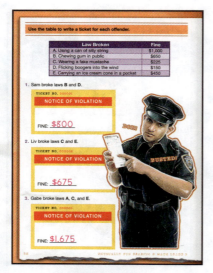
Page 82

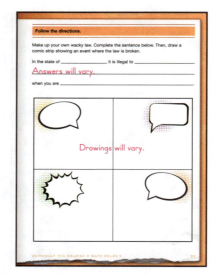
Page 83

Answer Key

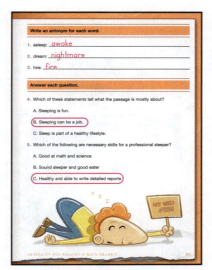

Page 85

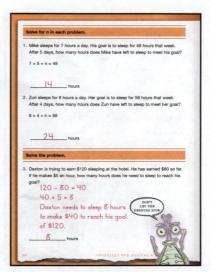

Page 86

Page 87

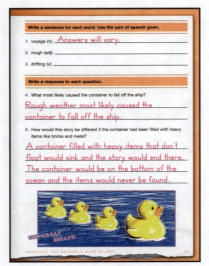

Page 89

Answer Key

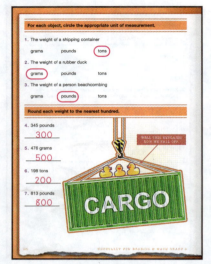
Page 90

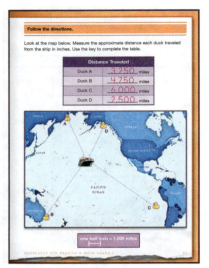
Page 91

Page 93

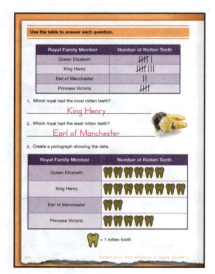
Page 94

Answer Key

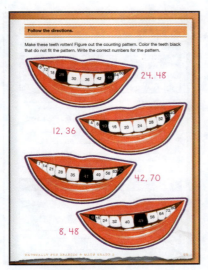
Page 95

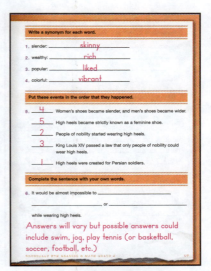
Page 97

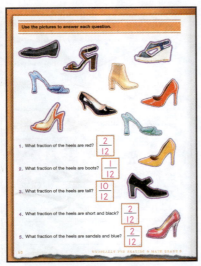
Page 98

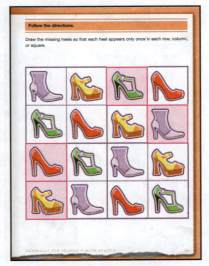
Page 99

Answer Key

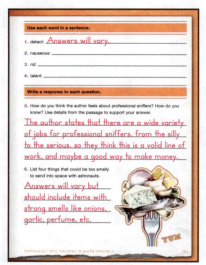

Page 101

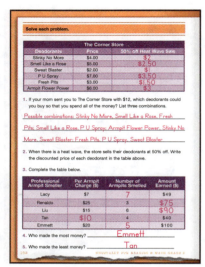

Page 102

Page 103

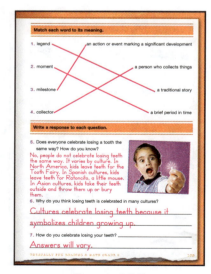

Page 105

Answer Key

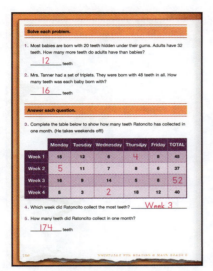

Page 106

Page 107

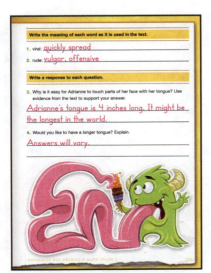

Page 109

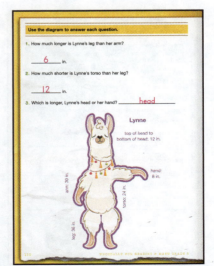

Page 110

Answer Key

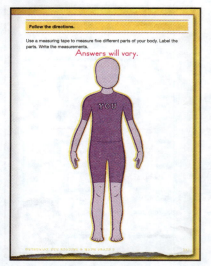

Page 111

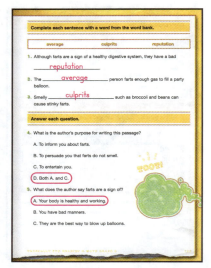

Page 113

Page 114

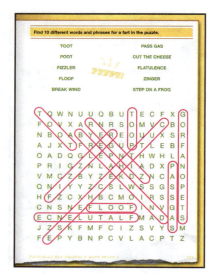

Page 115

Answer Key

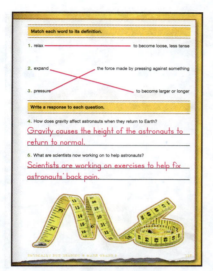

Page 117

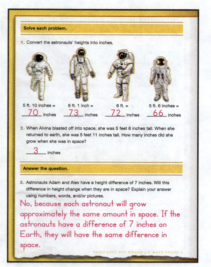

Page 118

Page 119

Page 121

Answer Key

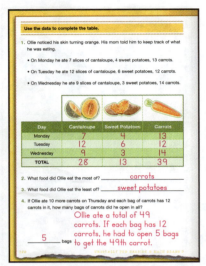
Page 122

Page 123

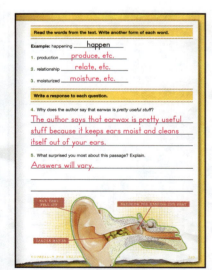
Page 125

Page 126

Answer Key

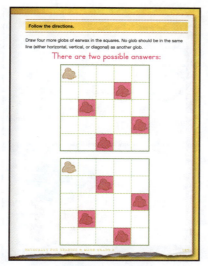

Page 127

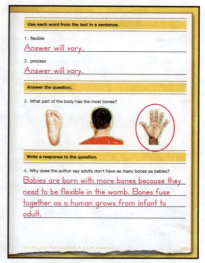

Page 129

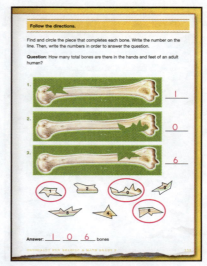

Page 130

Page 131

Answer Key

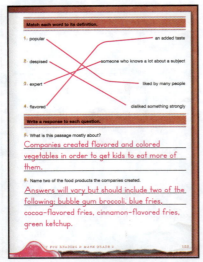

Page 133

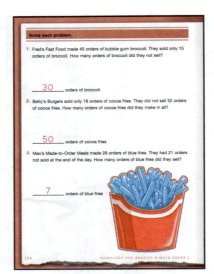

Page 134

Page 135

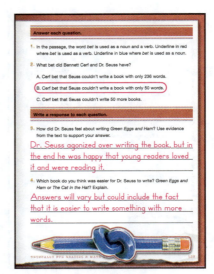

Page 137

Answer Key

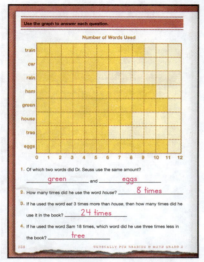

Page 138

Page 139

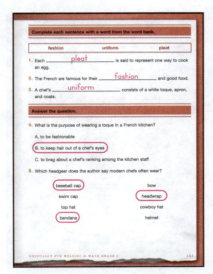

Page 141

Page 142

Answer Key

Page 143

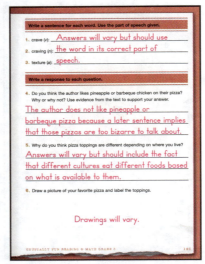

Page 145

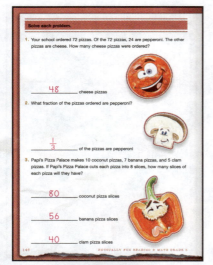

Page 146

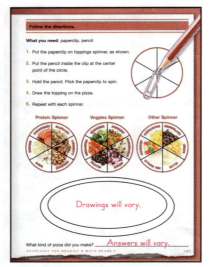

Page 147

Answer Key

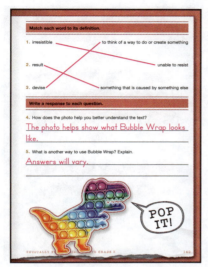
Page 149

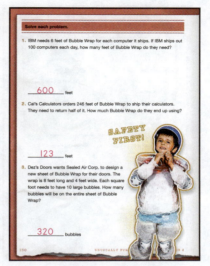
Page 150

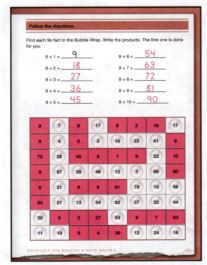
Page 151

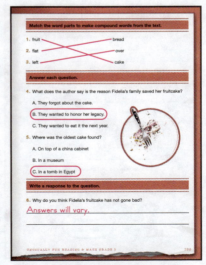
Page 153

Answer Key

Page 154

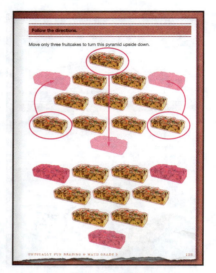

Page 155

Page 157

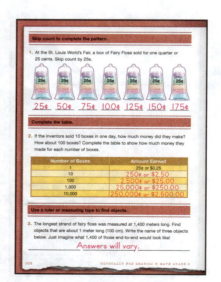

Page 158

Answer Key

Page 159

Page 161

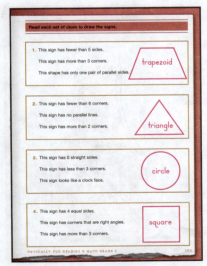

Page 162

Page 163

Answer Key

Page 165

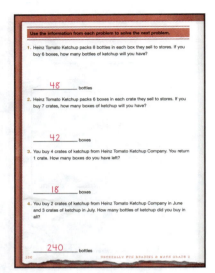

Page 166

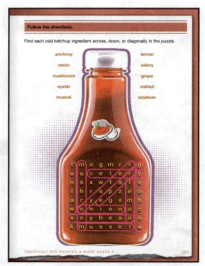

Page 167

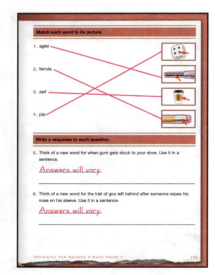

Page 169

Answer Key

Page 170

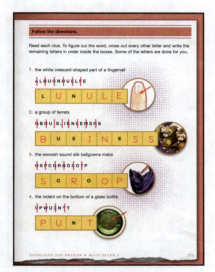
Page 171

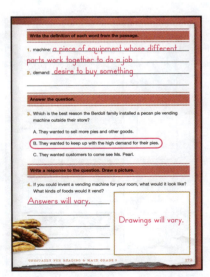
Page 173

Page 174

Answer Key

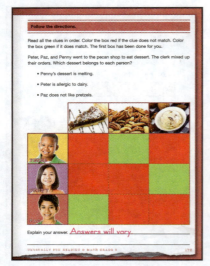

Page 175

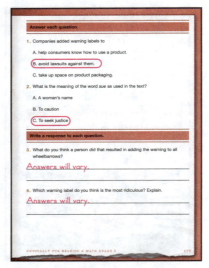

Page 177

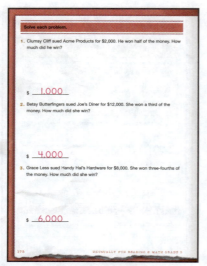

Page 178

Page 179

Answer Key

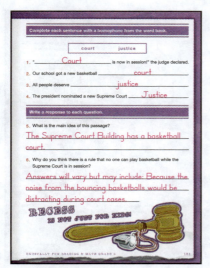

Page 181

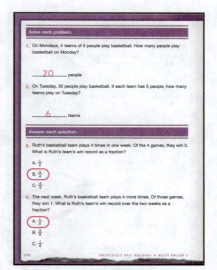

Page 182

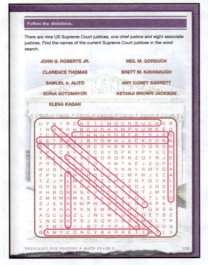

Page 183

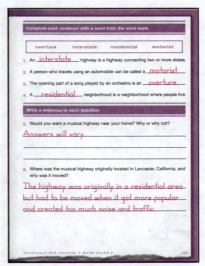

Page 185

Answer Key

Page 186

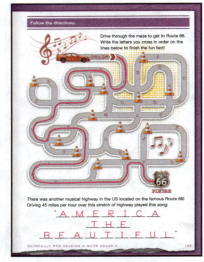

Page 187

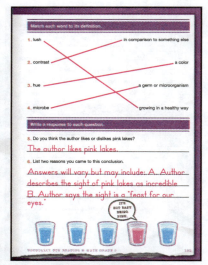

Page 189

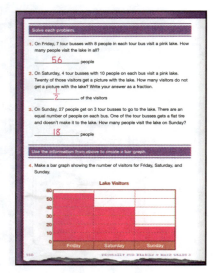

Page 190

Answer Key

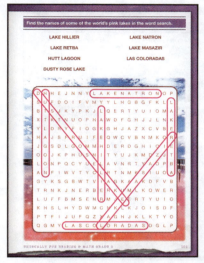

Page 191

Page 193

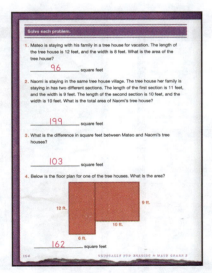

Page 194

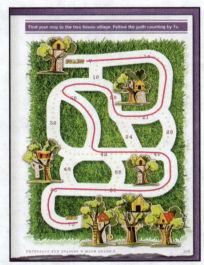

Page 195

Answer Key

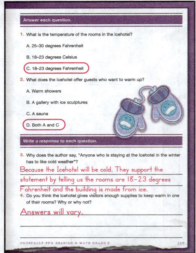
Page 197

Page 198

Page 199

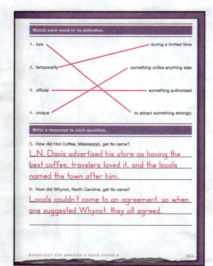
Page 201

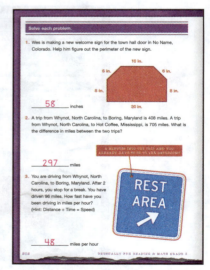
Page 202

Answer Key

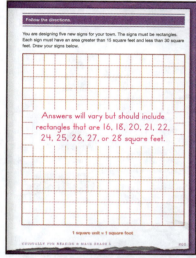
Page 203

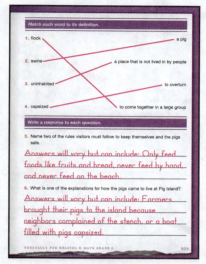
Page 205

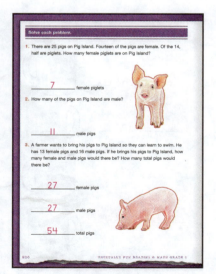
Page 206

Page 207

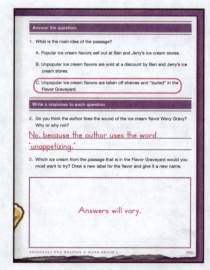
Page 209

Answer Key

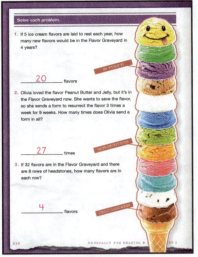

Page 210

Page 211

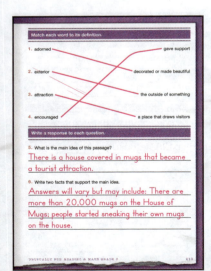

Page 213

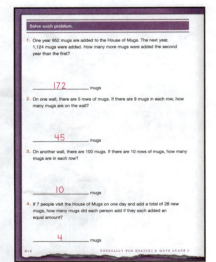

Page 214

Page 215